BECKET

or

THE HONOUR OF GOD

A Play in Four Acts

by

JEAN ANOUILH

Translated

by

LUCIENNE HILL

SAMUEL   FRENCH

LONDON

NEW YORK   TORONTO   SYDNEY   HOLLYWOOD

ISBN 0 573 01034 X

BECKET

Produced by the Royal Shakespeare Theatre Company at the Aldwych Theatre, London, on the 11th July 1961, with the following cast of characters—

(in the order of their appearance)

KING HENRY THE SECOND	*Christopher Plummer*
THOMAS BECKET	*Eric Porter*
A PAGE	*Philip Voss*
1ST SOLDIER	*Geoffrey Stavert*
2ND SOLDIER	*Stuart Hoyle*
THE ARCHBISHOP OF CANTERBURY	*Donald Layne-Smith*
THE BISHOP OF OXFORD	*P. G. Stephens*
THE BISHOP OF YORK	*Peter Russell*
GILBERT FOLLIOT, the Bishop of London	*Peter Jeffrey*
1ST BARON	*George Murcell*
2ND BARON	*Clive Swift*
3RD BARON	*Edward Argent*
4TH BARON	*Roy Dotrice*
SAXON FATHER	*Alan Downer*
SAXON GIRL	*Jeanne Hepple*
SAXON BOY	*Barry MacGregor*
GWENDOLEN	*Diana Rigg*
FRENCH GIRL	*Marion Diamond*
LITTLE MONK	*Ian Holm*
PROVOST MARSHAL	*Philip Voss*
FRENCH PRIEST	*P. G. Stephens*
FRENCH CHOIRBOY	*John Fox*
OFFICER	*Geoffrey Stavert*
1ST SERVANT	—
2ND SERVANT	—
QUEEN MOTHER	*Gwen Ffrangcon-Davies*
YOUNG QUEEN	*Yvonne Bonnamy*
PRINCES	{ *Dane Howell* { *John Fox*
ETIENNE	*Barry MacGregor*
ENGLISH PRIEST	—
1ST MONK	*Alan Downer*
2ND MONK	*Edward Argent*
KING LOUIS OF FRANCE	*Patrick Wymark*
1ST FRENCH BARON	*William Austin*
2ND FRENCH BARON	*Ian Cullen*
DUKE OF ARUNDEL	*James Keen*
THE POPE	*Roy Dotrice*
A CARDINAL	*George Murcell*
SENTRY	*Alan Downer*
YOUNG SENTRY	*Barry MacGregor*

Directed by PETER HALL
Settings by LESLIE HURRY

SYNOPSIS OF SCENES

ACT I

ACT II

ACT III

ACT IV

BECKET

ACT I

SCENE I

SCENE—*Canterbury Cathedral.*

A skeleton set with pillars and arches, which serve various purposes throughout the play. Becket's tomb is R, a stone slab with a name carved on it.

When the CURTAIN *rises, the stage is in darkness, then the lights come up on the area* C, *giving the effect of sunlight through stained-glass windows. Behind the pillars, in the shadows, one senses the disquieting presence of unseen lookers-on, and the faint murmur of a crowd is heard.* KING HENRY *enters up* L. *He is wearing his crown and is naked, except for his trousers and a big cloak. A* PAGE *follows at a distance. The* KING *moves slowly below the tomb, hesitates a moment, then removes his cloak with a swift movement. The* PAGE *quickly gathers up the cloak and exits with it up* L. *The* KING *falls to his knees on the stone floor, and prays, alone, in front of the tomb. The lights fade except for a spotlight on the King.*

KING. Well, Thomas Becket, are you satisfied? I am naked at your tomb and your monks are coming to flog me.

(*The crowd noises fade*)

What an end to our story. You, rotting in this tomb, larded with my Barons' daggers, and I, naked, shivering in the draught, and waiting like an idiot for those brutes to come and thrash me.

(BECKET, *in his Archbishop's robes, just as he was on the day of his death, enters in the shadows up* L)

Don't you think we'd have done better to understand each other?

(*A spotlight illuminates* BECKET, *who moves* LC)

BECKET (*softly*) Understand each other? It wasn't possible.
KING. I said, "In everything but the honour of the realm". It was you who taught me that slogan, after all.
BECKET. I answered you, "Everything but the honour of God." We were like two deaf men talking.
KING (*after a pause*) How cold it was on that bare plain at La Ferte Bernard, the last time we two met. It's funny, it's always been cold, in our story. Save at the beginning, when we

I

were friends. We had a few fine summer evenings together, with the girls. (*He pauses. Suddenly*) Did you love Gwendolen, Archbishop? Did you hate me, that night when I said, "I am the King", and took her from you. Perhaps that's what you never could forgive me for?

BECKET (*quietly*) I've forgotten.

KING. Yet we were like two brothers, weren't we—you and I? That night it was a childish prank—lusty lad shouting "I am the King!" I was so young. (*He pauses*) And every thought in my head came from you, you know that.

BECKET (*gently, as if to a little boy*) Pray, Henry, and don't talk so much.

KING (*irritably*) If you think I'm in the mood for praying at the moment . . .

> (*The spotlight fades on Becket.*
>   BECKET *quietly withdraws into the darkness and exits up* L *during the following speech*)

I can see them through my fingers, spying on me from the aisles. Say what you like, they're an oafish lot, those Saxons of yours. To give myself over naked to those ruffians! Me, with my delicate skin. Even you'd be afraid. Besides, I'm ashamed. Ashamed of this whole masquerade. I need them, though, that's the trouble. I have to rally them to my cause, against my son, who'll gobble up my kingdom if I let him. So I've come to make my peace with their Saint. You must admit it's funny. You've become a Saint and here am I, the King, desperately in need of that great Saxon mass which is all-powerful now. What use are conquests, when you stop to think? The Saxons are England, now, because of their vast numbers, and the rate at which they breed—like rabbits. But one must always pay the price—that's another thing you taught me, Thomas Becket, when you were still advising me. You taught me everything. (*He rises and removes his crown. Dreamily*) Ah, those were happy times. At the peep of dawn—well, our dawn that is, around noon, because we always went to bed very late—you'd come into my room, as I was emerging from the bathhouse, rested, smiling, debonair, as fresh as if we'd never spent the entire night drinking and whoring through the town. (*He moves down* C. *A little sourly*) That's another thing you were better at than me.

> The spotlight fades on the King and the general lighting comes up.

> The PAGE *enters* R *with a large white towel and the King's clothes. He puts the clothes on the stone slab down* R, *crosses to the King, wraps the towel around him, takes the crown from him and puts it on the stone slab. He then returns to the King and rubs him down with the towel.*

*The-*1ST SOLDIER *enters* R *with a brazier and logs which he sets down* C, *then exits* R. *Offstage is heard for the first time, we will hear it often,* BECKET *whistling, as he always does, a gay ironical Scottish marching song.*

SCENE 2

SCENE—*The King's room.*

BECKET *enters between the pillars up* LC. *He is dressed as a nobleman, elegant, young and charming in his short doublet and pointed, upturned shoes. He comes in blithely and greets the King.*

BECKET. My respects, my lord.

KING (*his face brightening*) Oh, Thomas—I thought you were still asleep.

BECKET (*moving above the brazier*) I've already been for a short gallop to Richmond and back, my Lord. There's a divine nip in the air.

KING (*his teeth chattering*) To think you actually like the cold. (*To the Page*) Rub harder, pig!

(BECKET, *smiling, pushes the Page aside and towels the King himself*)

(*To the Page*) Throw a log on the fire and get out. Come back and dress me later.

(*The* PAGE *puts a log in the brazier*)

BECKET. My prince, I shall dress you myself.

(*The* PAGE *runs off* L. BECKET *rubs the King's shoulders*)

KING. Nobody rubs me down the way you do.

(BECKET *slaps the King's sides*)

Thomas, what would I do without you?

(BECKET *rubs the King's arms*)

You're a nobleman, why do you play at being my valet? If I asked my Barons to do this, they'd start a civil war.

BECKET (*smiling*) They'll come round to it in time, when Kings have learnt to play their role.

(*They spar together for a few moments*)

I am your servant, my prince, that's all. Helping you to govern or helping you to get warm again is part of the same thing to me. I like helping you.

KING (*with an affectionate little gesture*) My little Saxon.

(BECKET *goes to the slab* R *and collects the King's shirt*)

At the beginning, when I told them I was taking you into my service, do you know what they all said? They said you'd knife me in the back one day.

BECKET (*moving to the King*) Did you believe them, my prince?

KING. N—no. I was a bit scared at first. You know I scare easily.

(BECKET *assists the King to put on his shirt*)

But you looked so well brought up, beside those brutes.

(BECKET *crosses to* R *and collects the King's coat*)

However did you come to speak French without a trace of an English accent?

BECKET. My parents were able to keep their lands by agreeing to "collaborate", as they say, with the King your father. They sent me to France as a boy to acquire a good French accent.

KING. To France? Not to Normandy?

BECKET (*smiling*) That was their one patriotic conceit. They loathed the Norman accent.

(BECKET *assists the king to put on his coat*)

KING (*distinctly*) Only the accent?

(BECKET *fastens the coat*)

BECKET (*lightly and inscrutably*) My father was a very severe man. I would never have taken the liberty of questioning him on his personal convictions. He managed, by collaborating, to amass a considerable fortune. As he was also a man of rigid principles, I imagine he contrived to do it in accordance with his conscience. That's a little piece of sleight of hand that men of principle are very adept at in troubled times. (*He moves to the stone slab down* R)

KING (*following Becket*) And you?

BECKET (*feigning not to understand the question*) I, my Lord? (*He bends over the slab to pick up the King's shoes*)

(*The* KING *puts a touch of contempt into his voice as he replies, for despite his admiration for Becket, or perhaps because of it, he would like to score a point against him occasionally*)

KING (*kicking Becket*) Were you adept at it, too? (*He sits on the slab*)

BECKET (*still smiling*) Mine was a different problem. I was a frivolous man, you'll agree? In fact, it never came up at all. (*He hands a shoe to the King*)

(*The* KING *puts on one shoe*)

I adore hunting and only the Normans and their protégés had the right to hunt. I adore luxury and luxury was Norman. I adore life and the Saxon's only birthright was slaughter. (*He hands the second shoe to the King*)

(*The* KING *puts on the second shoe*)

I'll add that I adore honour.

KING (*with faint surprise*) And honour was reconciled with collaboration, too?

BECKET (*lightly*) I had the right to draw my sword against the first Norman nobleman who tried to lay hands on my sister. I killed him in single combat. It's a detail, but it has its points.

KING (*a little slyly*) You could always have slit his throat and fled into the forest, as so many did. (*He puts on his belt*)

BECKET. That would have been uncomfortable, and not a lot of use. (*He moves above the brazier*) My sister would immediately have been raped by some other Norman baron, like all the Saxon girls. Today, she is respected.

(*The* KING *rises*)

(*Lightly*) My Lord, did I tell you? My new gold dishes have arrived from Florence. Will my Liege do me the honour of christening them with me at my house?

KING. Gold dishes! You lunatic!

BECKET. I'm setting a new fashion.

KING. I'm your King and I eat off silver!

BECKET (*moving to the King*) My prince, your expenses are heavy and I have only my pleasures to pay for. The trouble is, I'm told they scratch easily. We'll see. I received two forks, as well.

KING. Forks?

BECKET. Yes. It's a devilish little thing to look at—and to use, too. It's for pronging meat with and carrying it to your mouth. It saves you dirtying your fingers.

KING. But then you dirty the fork?

BECKET. Yes. But it's washable.

KING. So are your fingers. I don't see the point.

BECKET. It hasn't any, practically speaking.

(*The* KING *hits Becket*)

But it's refined, it's subtle. It's very un-Norman.

KING (*with sudden delight*) You must order me a dozen. (*He moves to the brazier*)

BECKET (*He laughs*) A dozen! Easy now, my lord. Forks are very expensive, you know.

KING. I want to see my great fat Barons' faces at the next Court banquet. We won't tell them what they're for. We'll have no end of fun with them.

BECKET (*collecting the King's crown*) My prince, it's time for the Privy Council. (*He puts the crown on the King's head*)

KING (*laughing*) They won't make head nor tail of them! I bet you they'll think they're a new kind of dagger. We'll have a hilarious time.

The KING *and* BECKET *exit* R, *laughing, as*—

the LIGHTS *dim to* BLACK-OUT

SCENE 3

SCENE—*The Council Chamber.*

There is a throne LC, *facing down* R, *and a seat* C, *facing down* L. *The stone slab remains down* R.

When the LIGHTS *come up, the* COUNCILLORS *are waiting. The* ARCH-BISHOP OF CANTERBURY *is sitting on the seat* C. *The* BISHOP OF OXFORD *is standing below the seat* C. GILBERT FOLLIOT, BISHOP OF LONDON, *is standing down* L. *He is a thin-lipped, venomous man. The* BISHOP OF YORK *is standing beside* FOLLIOT. *The* 1ST SOLDIER *is standing above the pillars* RC *and the* 2ND SOLDIER *is standing up* C. *The* KING *and* BECKET *enter up* R, *still laughing. The* KING *crosses and sits on the throne* LC. BECKET *goes to the stone slab down* R *and sits.*

KING. Gentlemen, the Council is open. I have summoned you here today to deal with this refusal of the clergy to pay the absentee tax. We really must come to an understanding about who rules this kingdom—the Church—

(*The* ARCHBISHOP *tries to speak*)

—just a moment, Archbishop—or me. But before we quarrel, let us take the good news first. I have decided to revive the office of Chancellor of England, Keeper of the Triple Lion Seal, and to entrust it to my loyal servant and subject—Thomas Becket.

(BECKET *rises in surprise, the colour draining from his face*)

BECKET. My Lord . . .

KING (*roguishly*) What's the matter, Becket? Do you want to go and pee already? True, we both had gallons to drink last night. (*He looks at Becket with delight*) Well, that's good! I've managed to surprise you for once, little Saxon.

(BECKET *moves* RC *and drops to one knee*)

BECKET (*gravely*) My Liege, this is a token of your confidence of which I fear I may not be worthy. I am very young, frivolous perhaps . . .

KING. I'm young, too. And you know more than all of us put together. (*To the others*) He's read books, you know. It's amazing the amount he knows. He'll checkmate the lot of you. Even the Archbishop. As for his frivolity, don't let him fool you. He drinks strong wine, he likes to enjoy himself, but he's a lad who thinks every minute of the time. Sometimes it embarrasses me to feel him thinking away beside me. Get up, Thomas.

(BECKET *rises*)

I never did anything without your advice, anyway. Nobody knew it, now everybody will, that's all. (*He bursts out laughing, pulls a seal from his pocket and tosses it to Becket*)

(BECKET *catches the seal*)

There. That's the Seal. Don't lose it. Without the Seal, there's no more England and we'll all have to go back to Normandy. (*He claps his hands*) Now, to work.

(*The* ARCHBISHOP *rises, all smiles, now the first shock is over*)

ARCHBISHOP. May I crave permission to salute, with my Lord's approval, my young and learned archdeacon here? For I was the first—I am weak enough to be proud of it—to notice him and take him under my wing. The presence at this Council of one of our brethren—our spiritual son in a sense, is a guarantee for the Church that a new era of mutual understanding is dawning for us all and we must now, in a spirit of confident co-operation . . .

KING (*interrupting*) Etcetera, etcetera. Thank you, Archbishop. I knew this nomination would please you.

(*The* ARCHBISHOP *resumes his seat*)

But don't rely too much on Becket to play your game. He is my man. (*He turns to Becket, beaming*) Come to think of it, I'd forgotten you were a deacon, little Saxon.

BECKET (*smiling*) So had I, my prince.

KING. Tell me—I'm not talking about wenching, that's a

venial sin—but on the odd occasions when I've seen you fight it seems to me you have a mighty powerful sword arm, for a priest. How do you reconcile that with the Church's commandment forbidding a priest to shed blood?

BISHOP OF OXFORD (*prudently*) Our young friend has not yet taken all his vows, my Lord. The Church in its wisdom knows that youth must have its day and that—under the sacred pretext of a war—a holy war, I mean, of course . . .

KING (*interrupting*) All wars are holy wars, Bishop. I defy you to find me a serious belligerent who doesn't have Heaven on his side, in theory. Let's get back to the point.

ARCHBISHOP. By all means, your Highness.

KING. Custom demands that every landowner, and that includes the Church, must send men-at-arms to the quarterly review of troops, fully armed and sword in hand, or pay a tax in silver. Where is my tax?

BISHOP OF OXFORD. *Distingo*, your Highness.

KING. Distinguish as much as you like. I've made up my mind. I want my money. My purse is open, just drop it in. (*He sprawls back in his throne and picks his teeth. To Becket*) Thomas, I don't know about you, but I'm starving. Have them bring us something to eat.

> (BECKET *signs to the 1st Soldier*
> *The* 1ST SOLDIER *exits* R. *There is a pause.* BECKET *crosses above the pillars and stands up* R *of the throne*)

ARCHBISHOP. A layman who shirks his duty to the State, which is to assist his Prince with arms, should pay the tax. Nobody will question that.

KING (*jovially*) Least of all the clergy.

ARCHBISHOP. A churchman's duty is to assist his Prince in his prayers, and in his educational and charitable enterprises. He cannot therefore be liable to such a tax unless he neglects those duties.

BISHOP OF OXFORD. Have we refused to pray?

> (*The* KING *rises in a fury, takes a step forward then kicks the base of the throne*)

KING. Do you seriously think that I am going to let myself be swindled out of more than two-thirds of my revenues with arguments of that sort? (*He turns to Becket*) Come on, Chancellor, say something. Has your new title caught your tongue?

BECKET (*moving to* R *of the King*) May I respectfully draw my Lord Archbishop's attention to one small point?

KING (*grunting*) Respectfully, but firmly. You're the Chancellor now.

BECKET (*calmly and casually*) England is a ship.

KING (*beaming*) Why, that's neat. We must use that, some time.

BECKET. In the hazards of sea-faring, the instinct of self-preservation has always told men that there must be one— (*He puts a hand on the King's shoulder*) and only one Captain on board ship.

ARCHBISHOP. My Lord Chancellor—the Captain is sole master after God. (*He thunders suddenly, with a voice one did not suspect from that frail body*) After God! (*He crosses himself*)

(*The other* BISHOPS *cross themselves. The wind of excommunication shivers through the Council. The* KING, *awed, crosses himself*)

KING (*mumbling a little cravenly*) Nobody's trying to question God's authority, Archbishop.

BECKET (*who alone has remained unperturbed*) God steers the ship by inspiring the Captain's decisions. But I never heard tell that He gave His instructions directly to the helmsman.

(*The* KING *sits on the throne*)

FOLLIOT (*rising*) Our young Chancellor is only a deacon—but he is still a member of the Church. He cannot have forgotten that it is through the intermediary of our Holy Father the Pope and his Bishops—God's qualified representatives—that He dictates His decisions to men.

BECKET. There is a chaplain on board every ship, but he is not required to determine the size of the crew's rations, nor to take the vessel's bearings. My Reverend Lord the Bishop of London—who is the grandson of a sailor, they tell me, cannot have forgotten that point, either. (*He crosses down* R *and sits on the stone slab*)

FOLLIOT (*yelping*) I will not allow personal insinuations to compromise the dignity of a debate of this importance! The integrity and honour of the Church are at stake!

KING (*cheerfully*) No big words, Bishop. You know as well as I do that all that's at stake is its money. I need money for my wars. Will the Church give me any, yes or no?

ARCHBISHOP. Your Highness, I am here to defend the privileges which your illustrious forefather William granted to the Church in England. Would you have the heart to tamper with your forefather's work?

KING. May he rest in peace.

(*The* ARCHBISHOP *crosses himself*)

His work is inviolable. But where he is now he doesn't need money. I'm still on earth unfortunately, and I do.

FOLLIOT (*moving* L *of the throne*) Your Highness, this is a question of principle.

KING. I'm levying troops, Bishop. I have sent for three thousand Swiss infantry to help fight the King of France. And nobody has ever paid the Swiss with principles.

BECKET (*rising suddenly and crossing to* C; *incisively*) I think, your Highness, that it is pointless to pursue a discussion in which neither speaker is listening to the other. The law and custom of the land give us the means of coercion. We will use them.

FOLLIOT (*moving towards Becket; beside himself*) Would you dare to plunge a dagger in the bosom of your Mother Church?

BECKET. My Lord and King has given me his Seal with the Three Lions to guard. My mother is England now.

FOLLIOT (*frothing, and slightly ridiculous*) A deacon! A miserable deacon nourished in our bosom. Traitor! (*He moves to* L *of the throne*) Little viper! Libertine! Sycophant! Saxon!

KING (*rising*) My Reverend friend, I suggest you respect my Chancellor— (*He raises his voice a little*) or else I'll call my guards.

(*The* 1ST SOLDIER *enters* R *with a tray of food and moves down* RC)

(*Surprised*) Why, here they are. Oh, no, it's my snack. Excuse me, gentlemen— (*He crosses to the Soldier and takes some food*) but around noon I need something to peck at or I tend to feel weak. And a King mustn't weaken, I needn't tell you that. I'll have it in my chapel, then I can pray directly afterwards.

(*The* SOLDIER *crosses and exits with the tray up* L)

(*To Becket*) Come and sit with me, son.

(*The* ARCHBISHOP *rises.*
The KING *kisses the Seal and exits with* BECKET *up* L. *The* BISHOPS, *deeply offended, move together* C *and murmur to one another with sidelong glances after the King*)

FOLLIOT. We must appeal to Rome. We must take a firm line.

YORK. My Lord Archbishop, you are the Primate of England. You have a weapon against such intransigeance: excommunication.

BISHOP OF OXFORD. We must not use it save with a great deal of prudence, Reverend Bishop. Let us bide our time. The King's rages are terrible, but they don't last. They are fires of straw.

FOLLIOT (*crossing to* R) The little self-seeker he has at his elbow now will make it his business to kindle them.

(BECKET *enters up* L *and crosses to* C)

BECKET. My Lords, the King has decided to adjourn his Privy Council. He thinks that a night of meditation will inspire your

Lordships with a wise and equitable solution—which he author-
izes you to come and submit to him tomorrow.

FOLLIOT (*with a bitter laugh*) You mean it's time for the hunt.

BECKET (*moving down* C; *smiling*) Yes, my Lord Bishop, to be
perfectly frank with you, it is. Believe me, I am personally most
grieved at this difference of opinion, but I cannot go back on
what I said as Chancellor of England. We are all bound, laymen
as well as priests, by the same feudal oath we took to the King
as our Lord and Sovereign; the oath to preserve his life, limbs,
dignity and honour. None of you, I think, has forgotten the words
of that oath? (*He moves* RC)

ARCHBISHOP (*moving to* L *of Becket; quietly*) We have not forgotten it, my son. No more than the other oath we took, before
that—the oath to God. You are young, and still uncertain of
yourself, perhaps. Yet you have, in those few words, taken a
resolution the meaning of which has not escaped me. Will you
allow an old man, who is very close to death, and who, in this
rather sordid argument was defending more perhaps than you
suspect—to hope, as a father, that you will never know the bitter-
ness of realizing, one day, that you made a mistake. (*He holds out
his ring*)

(BECKET *kneels and kisses the ring*)

I give you my blessing, my son.

BECKET (*lightly*) An unworthy son, Father, alas. (*He rises*) But
when is one worthy? And worthy of what?

(BECKET *pirouettes and exits up* L, *insolent and graceful as a young
boy*)

FOLLIOT (*moving to the Archbishop; violently*) Such insults to your
Grace cannot be tolerated. This young rake's impudence must be
crushed.

ARCHBISHOP (*thoughtfully*) He was with me for a long time.
His is a strange, elusive nature. Don't imagine he is the ordinary
libertine that outward appearances would suggest. I've had
plenty of opportunity to observe him. He is as it were detached.
As if seeking his real self.

FOLLIOT. Break him, my Lord, before he finds it. Or the clergy
of this country will pay dearly.

ARCHBISHOP. We must be circumspect. Our task is to see into
the hearts of men. And I am not sure that this one will always be
our enemy.

The four BISHOPS *exit* L *as*—

the LIGHTS *dim to* BLACK-OUT

Scene 4

Scene—*A forest.*

The pillars are RC, *topped by branches lowered from the flies. They are backed by a clear sky, transforming them into the leafless trees of a forest in winter.*

When the Lights *come up, the stage is empty. The sound of hunting-horns is heard. The four* Barons *enter* L, *ride across the stage and exit* R. *This is effected by means of richly caparisoned "hobby horses". The* King *and* Becket, *similarly "mounted" enter down* R *and cross to* C. *Each has a hawk on his gauntleted wrist. There is a peal of thunder and the sound of torrential rain.*

King. Here comes the deluge.

    (*There is a peal of thunder*)

(*Unexpectedly*) Do you like hunting this way, with hawks?

    (*The sound of the rain fades slightly*)

Becket. I don't much care to have my work done for me; I prefer to feel a wild boar on the end of my spear. When he turns and charges there's a moment of delicious personal contact when one feels, at last, responsible for oneself.

King. It's odd, this craving for danger. Why are you all so hell bent on risking your necks for the most futile reasons?

Becket. One has to gamble with one's life to feel alive.

King. Or dead! You make me laugh. I'll tell you one creature that loves hawking, anyway, and that's a hawk. It seems to me we've rubbed our backsides sore with three hours' riding just to give them this royal pleasure.

Becket (*smiling*) My Lord, these are Norman hawks. They belong to the master race. They have a right to it.

    (*The sound of the rain ceases*)

King (*suddenly, as he reins his horse*) Do you love me, Becket?

Becket. I am your servant, my prince.

King. Did you love me when I made you Chancellor? I wonder sometimes if you're capable of love. Do you love Gwendolen?

Becket. She is my mistress, my prince.

King. Why do you put labels on to everything to justify your feelings?

Becket. Because, without labels, the world would have no shape, my prince.

King. Is it so important for the world to have a shape?

    (*The sound of the rain recommences*)

BECKET. It's essential, my prince, otherwise we can't know what we're doing. The rain is getting heavier, my Lord. Come, we can shelter in that hut over there.

(BECKET *gallops off down* L.
The KING, *after a second of confused indecision, gallops off after Becket, holding his hawk high*)

KING (*as he goes; shouting*) Becket! You didn't answer my question.

The sound of the hunting-horns is heard.

The four BARONS *gallop on* R, *cross and exit down* L. *There is a flash of lightning and a peal of thunder as—*

the LIGHTS *dim to* BLACK-OUT

SCENE 5

SCENE—*A Saxon hut.*

A corner of the hut is seen, set LC. *The entrance is* L. *There is a pile of rags against the wall* R.

When the LIGHTS *come up, the hut is apparently empty, but the* SAXON GIRL *is concealed under the pile of rags. The sound of the rain ceases.*

BECKET (*off; shouting*) Hey, there! You! Fellow! Can we put the horses under cover in your barn? Do you know how to rub down a horse? We'll sit out the storm under your roof.

(*The* KING *enters the hut, followed by* BECKET *and a hairy* SAXON *who, cap in hand, bows repeatedly in terrified silence as he moves down* R. BECKET *stands up* C)

KING (*moving down* L *and shaking himself*) What a soaking! I'll catch my death. (*He sneezes*) All this just to keep the hawks amused. (*He shouts at the man*) What are you waiting for? Light a fire, dog! It's freezing cold in this shack.

(*The* MAN, *terror-stricken, does not move*)

(*He sneezes. To Becket*) What is he waiting for?

BECKET. Wood is scarce, my Lord. I don't suppose he has any left.

KING. What—in the middle of the forest?

BECKET. They are entitled to two measures of dead wood. One branch more and they're hanged.

KING (*astounded*) Really? And yet people are always complaining about the amount of dead wood in the forests. Still, that's a problem for my stewards, not me. (*He shouts at the Man*)

Run and pick up all the wood you can carry and build us a roar-
ing fire. We won't hang you this time, dog.

(*The* Man, *terrified, dares not obey*)

Becket (*gently*) Go, my son. Your King commands it. You've
the right.

(*The* Man *crosses and exits, trembling and bowing repeatedly to the
ground*)

King. Why do you call that old man your son?

Becket. Why not? You call him dog, my prince.

King. It's a manner of speaking. Saxons are always called
"dog". I can't think why, really. One could just as well have
called them "Saxons". But that smelly old rag bag your son! (*He
sniffs*) What on earth can they eat to make the place stink so—
dung?

Becket. Turnips.

King. Turnips—what are they?

Becket. Roots.

King (*amused*) Do they eat roots?

Becket. Those who live in the forests can't grow anything
else.

King. Why don't they move out into the open country, then?

Becket. They would be hanged if they left their district.

King. Oh, I see. Mark you, that must make life a lot simpler,
if you know you'll be hanged at the least show of initiative. They
don't know their luck. (*He moves to Becket*) But you still haven't
told me why you called the fellow your son?

Becket (*lightly*) My prince, he is so poor and so bereft and I
am so strong beside him that he really is my son.

King. We'd go a long way with that theory.

Becket. Besides, my prince, you're appreciably younger than
I am and you call me "son" sometimes.

King. That's got nothing to do with it. It's because I love
you.

Becket. You are our King. We are all your sons and in your
hands.

King. What, Saxons, too?

Becket (*stripping off his gloves; lightly*) England will be fully
built when the Saxons are your sons as well.

King. You are a bore today. I get the feeling that I'm listening
to the Archbishop. And I'm dying of thirst. Hunt around and
see if you can't find us something to drink. Go on, it's your son's
house.

(Becket *looks quickly around then exits. The* King *looks around,
examining the hut with curiosity and touching things with grimaces of*

distaste. He looks at the heap of rags, then suddenly thrusts out his hand and pulls out the terrified SAXON GIRL)

(*He shouts*) Hey, Thomas! Thomas!

    (BECKET *enters*)

BECKET. Have you found something to drink, Lord?

KING (*holding the Girl at arm's length*) No, something to eat. (*He pushes the Girl down* L) What do you say to that, if it's cleaned up a bit?

BECKET (*coldly*) She's pretty.

KING (*moving to* R *of Becket*) She stinks a bit, but we could wash her. Look, did you ever see anything so tiny? How old would you say it was—fifteen, sixteen?

BECKET (*quietly*) It can talk, my Lord. (*To the Girl. Gently*) How old are you?

    (*The* GIRL *looks at them in terror and says nothing*)

KING. You see? Of course it can't talk.

    (*The* MAN *enters with a load of wood and stops in the doorway, terrified*)

How old is your daughter, dog?

    (*The* MAN *trembles like a cornered animal and says nothing*)

He's dumb as well, that son of yours. How did you get him—with a deaf girl?

    (*The* MAN *moves down* L)

It's funny the amount of dumb people I meet the second I set foot out of my palace. I rule over a kingdom of the dumb.

    (*The* GIRL *creeps across to* R)

Can you tell me why?

BECKET. They're afraid, my prince.

    (*The* MAN *puts the wood on the floor down* L *and kneels beside it*)

KING. I know that. And a good thing, too. The populace must live in fear—it's essential. The moment they stop being afraid they have only one thought in mind—to frighten other people instead. Give them a chance to do it and they catch up fast, those sons of yours. (*He moves to* R *of the Man and looks at him. Exasperated*) Look at it, will you? It's tongue-tied, it's obtuse, it stinks and the country is crawling with them.

    (*The* GIRL *sneaks behind the King towards the door*)

(*He swings round on the girl*) Stay there, you.

(*The* GIRL *crouches on the floor down* LC)

(*To Becket*) I ask you, what use is it?

BECKET (*smiling*) It scratches the soil, it makes bread.

KING. Bread, in a land of beef-eaters—I never touch the stuff.

BECKET (*smiling*) The troops have to be fed. For a King without troops . . .

KING (*struck by this*) True enough! Yes, that makes sense. Well, well, you little Saxon philosopher, you. (*He moves to Becket*) I don't know how you do it, but you'll turn me into an intelligent man yet. The odd thing is, it's so ugly and yet it makes such pretty daughters. How do you explain that, you who can explain it all?

BECKET. At twenty, before he lost his teeth and took on that indeterminate age the common people have, that man may have been handsome. He may have had one night of love, one minute when he, too, was a King, and shed his fear. Afterwards, his pauper's life went on, eternally the same. And he and his wife no doubt forgot it all. But the seed was sown.

KING (*dreamily*) You have such a way of telling things. (*He looks at the Girl*) Do you think she'll grow ugly, too?

BECKET. For sure.

KING (*moving to the Girl*) If we made her a whore and kept her at the palace, would she stay pretty?

BECKET. Perhaps.

KING. Then we'd be doing her a service, don't you think?

BECKET (*coldly*) No doubt.

(*The* MAN *stiffens. The* GIRL *cowers in terror.*
The SAXON BOY *enters, sombre-faced, silent and threatening*)

KING. Would you believe it? They understand every word, you know. (*He looks at the Boy*) Who's that one there?

BECKET (*taking in the situation at a glance*) The brother.

KING. How do you know?

BECKET. Instinct, my Lord. (*His hand moves to his dagger*)

KING (*bawling suddenly*) Why are they staring at me like that? I've had enough of this. (*To the Man*) I told you to get us some water, dog.

(*The* MAN, *terrified, scuttles out. The* KING *moves down* L)

BECKET. Their water will be brackish. I have a gourd of juniper-juice in my saddle-bag. (*To the boy*) Come and give me a hand, you. My horse is restive.

(BECKET *seizes the Boy roughly by the arm and hustles him out of the hut. They cross behind the hut to* RC, BECKET *carelessly whistling his little marching song. The* KING *settles himself on the floor down* L *of the hut, whistling to himself. The* BOY *suddenly draws a knife and hurls himself on Becket. There is a short, silent struggle.* BECKET *gets the knife from the Boy.*

The BOY *escapes and runs off up* R. BECKET *watches him for a second, holding his wounded hand, then he exits above the hut*)

KING (*in a murmur*) All my sons! (*He shakes himself*) That Becket! He wears me out. He keeps making me think. I'm sure it's bad for the health. (*He lifts the Girl's skirts with his riding-crop and examines her at leisure*)

(BECKET *enters, carrying a small gourd. His hand is wrapped in a bloodstained cloth.*

The MAN *follows Becket on, carrying a bowl of water*)

What about that water? How much longer do I have to wait?

BECKET. Here it is, my Lord. But it's dirty. Have some of this juniper-juice instead. (*He hands the gourd to the King*)

(*The* KING *drinks and returns the gourd to Becket*)

KING. Drink with me. (*He notices Becket's hand*) What's the matter? You're wounded! (*He rises*)

BECKET (*hiding his hand*) No doubt about it, that horse of mine is a nervous brute. (*He crosses to* R) He can't bear his saddle touched. He bit me.

KING (*with a hearty, delighted laugh*) That's funny. Oh, that's very funny. Milord is the best rider in the kingdom.

(BECKET *drinks*)

Milord makes us all look silly at the jousts, with his fancy horse-manship, and when he goes to open his saddle-bags he gets him-self bitten. (*He moves to Becket*) Like a page. (*He is almost savagely gleeful, then suddenly his gaze softens*) You're white as a sheet, little Saxon. Why do I love you? It's funny, I don't like to think of you in pain. Show me that hand. A horse bite can turn nasty. I'll put some of that juniper gin on it. (*He grips Becket's hand*)

BECKET (*snatching his hand away*) I already have, my lord, it's nothing.

KING. Then why do you look so pale? Show me your hand.

BECKET (*with sudden coldness*) It's an ugly wound and you know you hate the sight of blood.

KING (*stepping back a little and exclaiming with delight*) All this just to fetch me a drink. Wounded in the service of the King. We'll tell the others you defended me against a wild boar and I'll present you with a handsome gift this evening. What would you like?

BECKET (*softly*) This girl. (*He pauses*) I fancy her.

(*There is a pause. The* KING'S *face clouds over*)

King. That's tiresome of you. I fancy her, too. And where that's concerned, friendship goes by the board. (*He pauses and his face takes on a cunning look*) All right, then. But favour for favour. You won't forget, will you?

Becket. No, my prince.

King. Favour for favour; do you give me your word as a gentleman?

Becket. Yes, my prince.

King (*suddenly cheerful*) Done! She's yours. Do we take her with us or shall we have her sent?

Becket. I'll send two soldiers to fetch her.

(*The* Barons *are heard shouting off* l)

Listen. The others have caught up.

King (*to the Man*) Wash your daughter, dog, and kill her fleas. She's going to the palace. For Milord here, who's a Saxon, too. You're pleased about that, I hope? (*He moves to the door and turns to Becket*) Give him a gold piece. I'm feeling generous this morning.

(*The* King *exits. The* Man *looks at Becket in terror*)

Becket. No one will come and take your daughter away. Keep her better hidden in future. And tell your son to join the others, in the forest, he'll be safer there, now. I think one of the soldiers saw us. (*He takes out a purse*) Here!

(Becket *throws the purse to the Man and exits. When he has gone the* Man *snatches up the purse, then spits venomously, his face twisted with hate*)

Man. God rot his guts! Pig!

Girl (*unexpectedly*) He was handsome, that one. Is it true he's taking me to the palace?

Man. You whore. (*He picks up a stick*) You Norman trollop. (*He hurls himself on to the Girl and savagely beats her*)

The sound of the hunting-horns is heard as—

the Lights *dim to* Black-out

Scene 6

Scene—*Becket's Palace.*

A candelabrum is set near one of the pillars. There is a low bed-couch with cushions on it down l. *A tapestry up* lc, *may hang across from* l *to* c.

When the LIGHTS *come up, singing and roars of laughter are heard off up* L *from the* BARONS *and banqueting guests.* GWENDOLEN *is curled up on the couch, playing a stringed instrument.* BECKET *enters up* L *and moves to Gwendolen, while the banqueting and the laughter, punctuated by hoarse incoherent snatches of song, continue.* GWENDOLEN *stops playing)*

GWENDOLEN. Are they still eating?
BECKET. Yes. (*He kneels beside Gwendolen*) They have an unimaginable capacity for absorbing food.

(*They embrace and kiss*)

GWENDOLEN (*softly*) How can my Lord spend his days and a large part of his nights with such creatures?
BECKET (*crouching at her feet and caressing her*) If he spent his time with learned clerics debating the sex of angels, your Lord would be even more bored, my kitten. They are as far from the true knowledge of things as these mindless brutes.
GWENDOLEN (*gently*) I don't always understand everything my Lord condescends to say to me. What I do know is that it is always very late when he comes to see me.
BECKET (*caressing her*) The only thing I love is coming to you. Beauty is the one thing which doesn't shake one's faith in God.
GWENDOLEN. I am my Lord's war captive and I belong to him body and soul. God has willed it so, since He gave the Normans victory over my people. If the Welsh had won the war I would have married a man of my own race, at my father's castle. God did not will it so.
BECKET (*quietly*) That belief will do as well as any, my kitten. But, as I belong to a conquered race myself, I have a feeling that God's system is a little muddled. Go on playing.

(GWENDOLEN *plays. The sounds from the banquet lessen*)

GWENDOLEN (*suddenly; gravely*) I'm lying. You are my Lord, God or no God. And if the Welsh had been victorious, you could just as easily have stolen me from my father's castle. I should have come with you.

(BECKET *turns away*)

(*She looks at him with anguished eyes and stops playing*) Did I say something wrong? What is the matter with my Lord?
BECKET. Nothing. I don't like being loved. I told you that.

(*The* KING *enters up* L. BECKET *and* GWENDOLEN *rise*)

KING (*a little drunk*) Well, son, have you deserted us? It worked! I told you. They're fighting with your forks. They've at last discovered that they're for poking one another's eyes out.

They think it's a most ingenious little invention. You'd better go in, son, they'll break them in a minute.

(BECKET *exits up* L. *The* KING *moves to Gwendolen and stares at her*)

BECKET (*off*) Gentlemen, gentlemen! No, no, they aren't little daggers. No, truly—they're for pronging meat. Look, let me show you again.

(*Huge roars of laughter are heard off*)

KING. Was that you playing, while we were at table?

GWENDOLEN (*with a deep curtsy*) Yes, my Lord.

KING. You have every kind of accomplishment, haven't you? Get up. (*He lifts her to her feet, caressing her as he does so*)

(*The sounds of banqueting fade.* GWENDOLEN *moves* C, *ill at ease*)

(*He moves behind Gwendolen. With a wicked smile*) Have I frightened you, my heart? We'll soon put that right. (*He moves up* L *and calls*) Hey there, Becket. That's enough horseplay, my fat lads. Come and hear a little music. When the belly's full, it's good to elevate the mind a bit. (*He turns to Gwendolen*) Play! Play!

(GWENDOLEN *picks up her instrument and sits on the right end of the couch. The* KING *sprawls on the couch, behind her.*
BECKET *enters up* L *and moves* C.
The four BARONS, *bloated with food and drink, follow Becket on. The* 1ST BARON *carries one of the new forks. He and the* 2ND BARON *sit at the base of the pillars. The* 3RD *and* 4TH BARONS *cross and sit on the floor down* R. *They all, with much sighing and puffing, unclasp their belts and soon fall into a stupor*)

(*To Becket*) Tell her to sing us something sad. I like sad music after dinner, it helps the digestion.

(BECKET *takes the fork from the 1st Baron*)

(*He hiccups*) You always feed us far too well, Thomas. Where did you steal that cook of yours?

BECKET (*moving and standing behind Gwendolen*) I bought him, Sire. He's a Frenchman.

KING. Really? Aren't you afraid he might poison you? (*He laughs*) Tell me, how much does one pay for a French cook?

(GWENDOLEN *plays*)

BECKET. A good one, like him, costs almost as much as a horse, my Lord.

KING (*genuinely outraged*) It's outrageous! What is the country coming to? No man is worth a horse. (*He takes the fork from Becket*) If I said "favour for favour"—remember—and I asked you to give him to me, would you?

BECKET. Of course, my Lord.

KING (*with a smile*) Well, I won't. I don't want to eat too well every day; it lowers a man's morale. (*He caresses Gwendolen with the fork*) Sadder, sadder, my little doe.

　　(BECKET *takes the fork and moves* C)

(*He sits up and belches*) Oh, that venison. Get her to sing that lament they composed for your mother, Becket. It's my favourite song.

BECKET. I don't like anyone to sing that lament, my Lord.

KING. Why not? Are you ashamed of being a Saracen girl's son? That's half your charm, you fool. There must be some reason why you're more civilized than all the rest of us put together. I adore that song.

　　(GWENDOLEN *looks uncertainly at Becket. There is a pause*)

(*Coldly*) That's an order, little Saxon.

BECKET (*to Gwendolen; inscrutably*) Sing.

　　(GWENDOLEN *strikes a few opening chords while the* KING *lies down and makes himself comfortable, belching contentedly.* BECKET *sits on the ground* C.)

GWENDOLEN (*singing*)
　　　　　Handsome Sir Gilbert
　　　　　Went to the war
　　　　　One fine morning in May
　　　　　To deliver the heart
　　　　　Of Lord Jesus our Saviour
　　　　　From the Saracens' sway.
　　　　　Woe! Woe! Heavy is my heart
　　　　　At being without love.
　　　　　Woe! Woe! Heavy is my heart
　　　　　All the livelong day.

KING and BARONS (*singing*)
　　　　　All the livelong day.

GWENDOLEN (*singing*)
　　　　　Fierce the battle raged
　　　　　And his great sword
　　　　　Slew many an infidel.
　　　　　But his trusty charger
　　　　　Stumbled in the fray
　　　　　And Sir Gilbert fell.
　　　　　Woe! Woe! Heavy is my heart
　　　　　At being without love.
　　　　　Woe! Woe! Heavy is my heart
　　　　　All the livelong day.

> Wounded in the head
> They led Gilbert the Brave
> To the Algiers market
> Chained hand and foot
> And sold him as a slave.

KING (*singing out of tune*)
> All the livelong day.

GWENDOLEN (*singing*)
> A Saracen's daughter
> Lovely as the night
> Lost her heart to him
> Swore to love him always
> Vowed to be his wife.
> Woe! Woe! Heavy is my heart
> At being without love.
> Woe! Woe! Heavy is my heart
> All the livelong day.

KING (*interrupting*) It brings tears to my eyes, you know, that story. I look a brute, but I'm soft as swansdown, really. One can't change one's nature. (*He sits up*) I can't imagine why you don't like people to sing that song. It's wonderful to be a love child. (*He rises and stands* R *of the couch*) When I look at my august parents' faces, I shudder to think what must have gone on. It's marvellous to think of your mother helping your father to escape and then coming to join him in London with you inside her. (*He moves and stands behind Gwendolen and puts his hands on her shoulders*) Sing us the end, girl. I adore the end.

GWENDOLEN (*singing softly*)
> Then he asked the holy Father
> For a priest to baptize her
> And he took her as his wife
> To cherish with his life
> Giving her his soul
> To love and keep alway
> Gay! Gay! Easy is my heart
> At being full of love
> Gay! Gay! Easy is my heart
> To be loved alway.

KING (*dreamily*) Did he really love her all his life? Isn't it altered a bit in the song?

BECKET, No, Sire.

KING (*moving* C; *quite saddened*) Funny, it's the happy ending that makes me feel sad. Do you believe in love, Thomas? (*He crosses to the pillars*)

BECKET (*coldly*) For my father's love for my mother, Sire, yes.

(*The* KING *crosses to* R, *kicking the snoring* BARONS *as he passes*)

KING. They've fallen asleep, the hogs. That's their way of showing their finer feelings. (*He moves up* C) You know, my little Saxon, sometimes I have the impression that you and I are the only sensitive men in England. We eat with forks and we have infinitely distinguished sentiments, you and I. You've made a different man of me, in a way. (*He moves and stands behind Gwendolen*) What you ought to find me now, if you loved me, is a girl to give me a little polish. I've had enough of whores. (*He puts his hand on Gwendolen's head and caresses her a little. Suddenly*) Favour for favour—do you remember?

(*There is a pause during which* BECKET *rises*)

BECKET (*pale*) I am your servant, my prince, and all I have is yours. But you were also gracious enough to say I was your friend.

KING (*sitting on the upstage side of the couch*) That's what I mean. As one friend to another, it's the thing to do. (*He pauses, smiles maliciously and caresses Gwendolen*)

(GWENDOLEN *cowers, terrified*)

You care about her, then? Can you care for something? Go on, tell me if you care about her?

(BECKET *is silent*)

(*He smiles*) You can't tell a lie. I know you. Not because you're afraid of lies—I think you must be the only man I know who isn't afraid of anything—not even Heaven—but because it's distasteful to you. You consider it inelegant. What looks like morality in you is nothing more than aesthetics. Is that true or isn't it?

BECKET (*meeting the King's eyes; softly*) It's true, my Lord.

KING. I'm not cheating if I ask for her, am I? I said "favour for favour" and I asked you for your word of honour.

BECKET (*icily*) And I gave it to you.

(*There is a pause. The* KING *looks at Becket with a wicked smile.* BECKET *does not look at the King*)

KING (*rising and moving briskly* R) Right. I'm off to bed.

(GWENDOLEN *rises*)

I feel like an early night tonight. Delightful evening, Becket. You're the only man in England who knows how to give your friends a royal welcome. (*He kicks the slumbering Barons*) Call my guards and help me wake these porkers.

(*The* Barons *wake with sighs and belches and rise*)

(*He pushes them about, shouting*) Come on, Barons, home. I know you're connoisseurs of good music, but we can't listen to music all night long. (*He crosses to Gwendolen, takes her hand and leads her* R) Happy evenings end in bed, eh, Becket?

Becket (*stiffly*) May I ask your Highness for a brief moment's grace?

King. Granted. Granted. I'm not a savage. I'll wait for you both in my litter. You can say good night to me downstairs.

(*The* King *exits* R.

The Barons, *singing, follow him off*. Becket *stands motionless for a while under* Gwendolen's *steady gaze*)

Becket (*crossing to* LC; *quietly*) You will have to go with him, Gwendolen.

Gwendolen (*composedly*) Did my Lord promise me to him?

Becket. I gave him my word of honour that I would give him anything he asked for. I never thought it would be you.

Gwendolen. If he sends me away tomorrow, will my Lord take me back?

Becket. No.

Gwendolen. Shall I tell the girls to put my dresses in the coffer?

Becket. He'll send over for it tomorrow. Go down. One doesn't keep the King waiting. Tell him I wish him a respectful good night.

Gwendolen. I shall leave my Lord my harp. He can almost play it now. (*She asks, quite naturally*) My Lord cares for nothing in the whole world, does he?

Becket. No.

Gwendolen (*moving to Becket; gently*) You belong to a conquered race, too. But through tasting too much of the honey of life, you've forgotten that even those who have been robbed of everything have one thing left to call their own.

Becket (*inscrutably*) Yes, I dare say you're right; I had forgotten. There is a gap in me where honour ought to be. Go now.

(Gwendolen *exits* R. Becket *stands quite still for a few moments, then pulls the fur coverlet from the bed, tosses it on the floor* C *and starts to unbutton his doublet*.

The 1st Soldier *enters* R, *dragging in the* Saxon Girl, *throws her on to the fur coverlet* C, *then moves and stands down* R.

The King *enters* R)

King (*hilariously*) Thomas, my son! You'd forgotten her. You

see how careless you are. Luckily, I think of everything. You see—
I really am a friend to you, and you're wrong not to love me. You
told me you fancied her. I hadn't forgotten that, you see. Sleep
well, son.

(*The* KING *picks up the candelabrum and exits* R.

The 1ST SOLDIER *follows him off. The* GIRL, *still dazed, rises,
looks at Becket, recognizes him*)

GIRL (*after a pause; with a kind of sly coquetry*) Shall I undress,
my Lord?

BECKET. Of course.

(*The* GIRL *starts to undress.* BECKET *looks at her, coldly, absent-
mindedly whistling a few bars of his little march. Suddenly he stops,
goes to the* GIRL, *who stands dazed and half naked, and seizes her by
the shoulders*)

I hope you're full of noble feelings and that all this strikes you as
pretty shabby?

(*The* KING *stumbles in* R.

The 1ST SOLDIER *follows him on.* BECKET *releases the Girl and
turns*)

KING (*soberly*) I had no pleasure with her, Thomas. She let
me lay her down in the litter, limp as a corpse, and then suddenly
she pulled out a little knife from somewhere. There was blood
everywhere. I feel quite sick. (*Haggard*) She could easily have
killed me instead. (*He pauses. Abruptly*) Send that girl away.

(BECKET *motions to the 1st Soldier.*

The 1ST SOLDIER *leads the half-naked Girl out* R)

(*He crosses to the couch*) I'm sleeping in your room tonight. I'm
frightened. (*He throws himself, fully dressed, on to the couch with an
animal-like sigh*) Take half the bed.

BECKET. I'll sleep on the floor.

KING. No. Lie down beside me. I don't want to be alone
tonight. (*He looks at Becket and murmurs*) You loathe me. I shan't
even be able to trust you now.

BECKET. You gave me your Seal to keep, my prince. And the
three lions of England which are engraved on it keep watch over
me, too.

KING (*his voice already thick with sleep*) I shall never know what
you're thinking.

BECKET. It will be dawn soon, my prince. (*He picks up the fur
coverlet from the floor and spreads it over the King*) You must sleep.
Tomorrow we are crossing to the Continent. (*He lies on the bed
alongside the King*) In a week we will face the King of France's
army and there will be simple answers to everything at last.

(*There is a pause during which the* King's *snoring gradually increases. Suddenly, the* King *moans and tosses in his sleep*)

King (*crying out*) They're after me. They're after me. Stop them! Stop them!

(Becket *sits up on one elbow. He touches the* King, *who wakes up with a great animal cry*)

Becket. My prince—my prince—sleep in peace. I'm here.
King. Oh—Thomas, it's you. They were after me. (*He turns over and goes back to sleep with a sigh. Gradually he begins to snore again, softly*)

(Becket *is still on one elbow. Almost tenderly he draws the coverlet over the King*)

Becket. My prince. If you were my true prince, if you were one of my race, how simple everything would be. How tenderly I would love you, then, my prince, in an ordered world. Each of us bound in fealty to the other, head, heart and limbs, with no further questions to ask of oneself, ever.

(*There is a pause. The* King's *snores grow louder*)

(*He sighs. With a little smile*) But I cheated my way in. An alien, a bastard, and stole my place among the conquerors. You can sleep peacefully, though, my prince. So long as Becket is obliged to improvise his honour, he will serve you. And if one day, he meets it face to face . . . (*He pauses briefly*) But where is Becket's honour?

Becket, *with a sigh, lies down. The* King's *snores grow louder still. The* Lights *grow dim as—*

the Curtain *falls*

ACT II

SCENE 1

SCENE—*A Forest in France.*

The pillars are topped by branches. There is a tent C, *which is the* KING'S. *It has exits both downstage and at the back of it. A bed is visible in the tent. A camp fire is down* C.

When the CURTAIN *rises, it is dawn. The tent is not yet open for the day. The four* BARONS *are crouched around the fire, having their morning meal in silence. The* 1ST BARON *is up* R *of the fire, the* 2ND BARON *is up* L *of it, the* 3RD BARON *is* R *of it and the* 4TH BARON *is* L *of it.*

After a while, the 1ST BARON *speaks.*

1ST BARON. This fellow Becket, then, who is he?

(*There is a pause. All four are fairly slow in their reactions*)

2ND BARON (*surprised at the question*) The Chancellor of England.

1ST BARON. I know that. But who is he, exactly?

2ND BARON. The Chancellor of England, I tell you. The Chancellor of England is the Chancellor of England. I don't see what else there is to enquire into on that score.

1ST BARON. You don't understand. Look, supposing the Chancellor of England were some other man. Me, for instance . . .

2ND BARON. That's plain idiotic.

1ST BARON. I said supposing. Now, I would be Chancellor of England, but I wouldn't be the same Chancellor of England as Becket is. You can follow that, can you?

2ND BARON. Yes.

1ST BARON. So, I *can* ask myself the question.

2ND BARON. What question?

1ST BARON. Who is this man Becket?

2ND BARON. What do you mean, who is this man Becket? He's the Chancellor of England.

1ST BARON. Yes. But what I'm asking myself is who is he, as a man?

2ND BARON (*looking at the 1st Baron; sorrowfully*) Have you got a pain?

1ST BARON. No, why?

2ND BARON. A Baron who asks himself questions is a sick Baron.

1ST BARON (*vexed*) I just meant I didn't like him, that's all.

2ND BARON. Why couldn't you say so, then? That we'd have

27

understood. I don't like him either, come to that. To begin with,
he's a Saxon.

1ST BARON. To begin with!

3RD BARON. One thing you can't say, though. You can't say
he isn't a fighter. Yesterday when the King was in the thick of it,
after his squire was killed, he cut his way right through the
French, and he seized the King's banner and drew the enemy off
and on to himself.

1ST BARON. All right. He's a good fighter.

3RD BARON (*to the 2nd Baron*) Isn't he a good fighter?

2ND BARON (*stubbornly*) Yes. But he's a Saxon.

1ST BARON (*to the 4th Baron*) How about you, Regnault? What
do you think of him?

4TH BARON (*swallowing his mouthful of food; placidly*) I'm
waiting.

1ST BARON. Waiting for what?

4TH BARON Till he shows himself. Some sorts of game are like
that you follow them all day sometimes through the forest. But it
wouldn't do any good to charge ahead with drawn lance, because
you don't know for sure what sort of animal it is you're dealing
with. You have to wait.

1ST BARON. What for?

4TH BARON. For whatever sort of animal it is you're dealing
with to show itself. And if you're patient it always does show itself
in the end. With this man Becket—I'll wait.

1ST BARON. What for?

4TH BARON. For him to show himself. For him to break cover.
(*He goes on eating*) The day he does, we'll know who he is.

(BECKET's *little whistled march is heard off.*
BECKET *enters* R *and crosses to* C. *He is armed*)

BECKET. Good morning to you, gentlemen.

(*The four* BARONS *rise politely*)

Is the King still asleep?

(*The* 3RD BARON *crosses to* L)

1ST BARON (*stiffly*) He hasn't called yet.

BECKET. Has the Camp Marshal presented his list of losses?

1ST BARON. No.

BECKET. Why not?

2ND BARON (*surlily*) He was part of the losses.

BECKET. Oh?

1ST BARON. I was nearby when it happened. A lance knocked
him off his horse. Once on the ground, the foot soldiers dealt
with him.

BECKET. Poor Beaumont. He was so proud of his new armour.

2ND BARON. There must have been a chink in it, then. They bled him white. On the ground. French swine!

BECKET (*with a light shrug*) That's war. The lesson of this battle, which has cost us far too much, is that we will have to form platoons of cut-throats, too, that's all.

1ST BARON. And a soldier's honour, my Lord Chancellor, what of that?

BECKET (*dryly*) A soldier's honour, my Lord Baron, is to win victories. I'll wake the King. Our entry into the city is timed for eight o'clock this morning and the *Te Deum* in the cathedral for a quarter past nine. It would be bad policy to keep the French Bishop waiting. We want these people to collaborate with a good grace.

1ST BARON (*grunting*) In my day, we slaughtered the lot and marched in afterwards.

BECKET. Yes, into a dead city. I want to give the King living cities to increase his wealth. From eight o'clock this morning, I am the French people's dearest friend.

1ST BARON. What about England's honour, my Lord Chancellor?

BECKET (*quietly*) England's honour, my Lord Baron, in the final reckoning, has always been to succeed.

(BECKET *exits into the King's tent* C, *smiling. The four* BARONS *look at each other, hostile*)

1ST BARON (*muttering*) What a mentality.

4TH BARON (*sententiously*) We must wait for him. One day he'll break cover.

(*The four* BARONS *exit down* L.
BECKET, *inside the tent, lifts the flap and hooks it back. The* KING *is revealed, in bed with a* FRENCH GIRL. *The* GIRL *laughs*)

KING (*yawning*) Good morning, son.

(*The* GIRL *sits up*)

Did you sleep well?

BECKET (*moving to* L *of the bed*) A little memento from the French on my left shoulder kept me awake, Sire. I took the opportunity to do some thinking.

KING. What do you think of my little French girl? I must say, I adore France.

(*The* GIRL *giggles*)

BECKET (*smiling*) So do I, Sire, like all Englishmen.

KING. The climate's warm, the girls are pretty, the wine is

good. I intend to spend at least a month here every winter. (*He caresses the Girl*)

BECKET. The only snag is, it's expensive. Two thousand casualties yesterday. My prince, shall we get down to work? We haven't dealt with yesterday's despatches yet.

KING. Does it amuse you—working for the good of my people? Do you mean to say you love all those folk? To begin with, they're too numerous. One can't love them, one doesn't know them. Anyway, you're lying, you don't love anything or anybody.

BECKET (*tersely*) There's one thing I do love, my prince, and that I'm sure of. Doing what I have to do and doing it well.

KING (*sitting up; grinning*) Always the aes— aes— What's your word again?

BECKET (*smiling*) Aesthetics?

KING. Aesthetics! Always the aesthetic side, eh?

BECKET. Yes, my prince.

KING (*slapping the Girl's rump*) And isn't that aesthetic, too?

(*The* GIRL *giggles*)

Some people go into ecstasies over cathedrals. But this is a work of art, too. Look at that—round as an apple. (*Naturally, as if he were offering Becket a sweetmeat*) Want her?

BECKET (*smiling*) Business, my Lord.

KING (*pouting like a schoolboy*) All right. Business. (*He swings his feet out and sits on the right edge of the bed*) I'm listening. Sit down.

(BECKET *sits on the left edge of the bed, with the Girl like a fascinated rabbit between them*)

BECKET. The news is not good, my prince.

KING (*with a careless wave of the hand*) News never is. That's a known fact. Life is one long web of difficulties. The secret of it is to give them no importance whatever. In the long run one difficulty swallows up the other and you find yourself ten years later still alive with no harm done.

(*The* GIRL *embraces the King*)

Things always work out.

BECKET. Yes. But badly. My prince, when you play tennis, do you simply sit back and wait for the ball to hit your racquet, or do you . . . ?

KING. Ah, now just a minute. A game of tennis is important, it amuses me. (*He picks up his shirt and puts it on*)

BECKET. But governing can be just as amusing as a game of tennis. Are we going to let them smash the ball into our court, my prince, or shall we try to score a point, like two good English sportsmen?

KING (*suddenly roused by his sporting instinct*) The point, begod, the point! You're right. On the court I fall over my feet, I half kill myself, I'll cheat if need be, but I never give up the point.

BECKET. Well then, I'll tell you what the score is, so far. Piecing together all the information I have received from London since we've been on the Continent, one thing strikes me, and that is: that there exists in England a power which has grown until it almost rivals yours, my Lord. It is the power of your clergy.

KING. We did get them to pay the tax. That's something.

BECKET. Yes, it's a small sum of money. And they know that princes can always be pacified with money. But those men are past-masters at taking back with one hand what they were forced to give with the other. That's a little conjuring trick they've had centuries of practice in.

KING (*to the Girl*) Pay attention, my little sparrow. Now's your chance to educate yourself. The gentleman is saying some very profound things.

BECKET (*rising; in the same flippant way*) Little French sparrow, suppose you educate us instead. When you're married—if you do marry despite the holes in your virtue—which would you prefer, to be mistress in your own kitchen or to have your village priest laying down the law there?

KING. Talk sense, Becket. Priests are always intriguing, I know that. But I also know that I can crush them any time I like.

BECKET. Talk sense, Sire. If you don't do the crushing now, in five years' time there will be two Kings in England, the Archbishop of Canterbury and you. And in ten years' time there will be only one.

KING (*a bit shamefaced*) And it won't be me?

BECKET (*coldly*) I rather fear not.

KING (*with a sudden shout*) Oh, yes, it will. (*He rises, picks up the blanket and throws it over the Girl*) We Plantagenets hold on to our own. To horse, Becket, to horse! For England's glory.

(*The* GIRL *emerges, dishevelled and red in the face*)

GIRL (*pleadingly*) My Lord! I can't breathe.

(*The* KING *looks at the Girl in surprise. He had clearly forgotten her. He bursts out laughing*)

KING. What are you doing there? Spying for the clergy? Be off. Put your clothes on and go home. (*He rolls the Girl out of the bed*) Give her a gold piece, Thomas.

(*The* GIRL *picks up her rags and holds them up in front of her*)

GIRL. Am I to come back to the camp tonight, my Lord?

KING (*exasperated*) Yes. No. I don't know. We're concerned with the Archbishop now, not you. Be off.

(The GIRL exits at the back of the tent)

To horse, Thomas! For England's greatness. With my big fist and your big brain we'll do some good work, you and I. *(With sudden concern)* Wait a second. You can never be sure of finding another one as good in bed. *(He goes to the entrance at the rear of the tent and shouts)* Come back tonight, my angel. I adore you. You have the prettiest eyes in the world. *(He moves to Becket. Confidentially)* You always have to tell them that, even when you pay for it, if you want real pleasure with them. That's high politics, too. *(Suddenly anxious, as his childish fear of the clergy returns)* What will God say to it all, though? After all, they're *His* bishops.

BECKET *(with an airy gesture)* We aren't children. You know one can always come to some arrangement with God, on this earth. Make haste and dress, my prince. We're going to be late.

KING. I'll be ready in a second. Do I have to shave?

BECKET *(smiling)* It might be as well, after two days fighting.

KING. What a fuss for a lot of conquered Frenchmen. I wonder sometimes if you aren't a bit too finicky, Thomas.

(BECKET comes from the tent and closes the flap.
    The two SOLDIERS enter R, bringing on a YOUNG MONK, with his hands tied. They cross to C)

BECKET. What is it?

1ST SOLDIER. We've just arrested this young monk, my Lord. He was loitering round the camp. He had a knife under his robe. We're taking him to the Provost.

BECKET. Have you got the knife?

(The 1ST SOLDIER hands a knife to BECKET, who looks at it and then at the little Monk)

What use do you have for this in your monastery?

MONK. I cut my bread with it.

BECKET *(amused)* Well, well. *(To the Soldiers)* Leave him to me. I'll question him.

1ST SOLDIER. He's turbulent, my Lord. It took four of us to tie him up. We'd have finished him there and then, only the Sergeant said there might be some information to be got out of him. That's why we're taking him to the Provost.

BECKET *(who has not taken his eyes off the little Monk)* Very well. Stand off.

(The SOLDIERS move out of earshot, up R)

(He goes on looking at the Monk, and playing with the knife) What are you doing in France? You're a Saxon.

MONK *(crying out despite himself)* How do you know?

BECKET. I can tell by your accent. I speak Saxon very well,

almost as well as you speak French. In your predicament, it would be as well to be taken for a Frenchman as a Saxon. It's less unpopular.

(*There is a pause*)

Monk (*abruptly*) I'm prepared to die.
Becket (*smiling*) After the deed. But before, you'll agree, it's stupid. (*He looks at the knife which he is holding between two fingers*) Where are you from?
Monk (*venomously*) Hastings.
Becket. Hastings. And who was this kitchen implement intended for?

(*The* Monk *is silent*)

You couldn't hope to kill more than one man with a weapon of this sort. You didn't make the journey for the sake of an ordinary Norman soldier, I imagine.

(*The* Monk *does not answer*)

(*Tersely*) Listen to me, my little man. They're going to put you to the torture. Have you ever seen that? One always talks. If I can vouch that you've made a full confession, it will go easier for you.

(*The* Monk *does not answer*)

Besides, there's an amusing detail to this affair. You are directly under my jurisdiction. The King gave me the deeds and livings of all the abbeys in Hastings when he made me Chancellor.
Monk. Are you Becket?
Becket. Yes. (*He looks at the knife and sniffs at it with faint distaste*) You didn't only use your knife to cut bread. It stinks of onion, like any proper little Saxon's knife. They're good, aren't they, the Hastings onions? (*He looks at the knife again with a strange smile*) You still haven't told me who it was for.

(*The* Monk *is silent*)

If you meant it for the King, there was no sense in that, my lad. He has three sons. Kings spring up again like weeds. Did you imagine you could liberate your race single-handed?
Monk. No. (*dully*) Not my race. Myself.
Becket. Liberate yourself from what?
Monk. My shame.
Becket (*with sudden gravity*) How old are you?
Monk. Sixteen.
Becket (*quietly*) The Normans have occupied the island for a

hundred years. Shame is a stale vintage. Your father and your grandfather drank it to the dregs. The cup is empty now.

MONK (*shaking his head*) No.

(*A shadow seems to cross* BECKET'S *eyes*)

BECKET (*quietly*) So, one fine morning, you woke in your cell to the bell of the first offices, while it was still dark. And it was the bells that told you, a boy of sixteen, to take the whole burden of shame on to yourself?

MONK (*with the cry of a cornered animal*) Who told you that?

BECKET (*indifferently*) I'm a Saxon, too, did you know that?

MONK (*stonily*) Yes.

BECKET (*smiling*) Go on. Spit. You're dying to.

(*The* MONK *looks at Becket, a little dazed, and then spits*)

(*He smiles*) That felt good, didn't it? (*Tersely*) The King is waiting. And this conversation could go on indefinitely. But I want to keep you alive, so we can continue it one of these days. (*Lightly*) It's pure selfishness, you know. Your life hasn't any sort of importance for me, obviously, but it's very rare for Fate to bring one face to face with one's own ghost, when young. (*He turns and calls*) Soldier.

(*The* 1ST SOLDIER *moves to Becket and springs clanking to attention*)

Fetch me the Provost. Run!

(*The* 1ST SOLDIER *runs out down* R)

(*He turns to the Monk*) Delightful day, isn't it? This early morning sun, hot already under this light veil of mist. A beautiful place, France. But I'm like you, I prefer the solid mists of the Sussex downs. Sunshine is luxury. And we belong to a race which used to despise luxury, you and I.

(*The* PROVOST MARSHAL *of the Camp enters down* R. *He is an important personage, but Becket is inaccessible, even for a Provost Marshal, and the man's behaviour shows it.*)

The 1ST SOLDIER *follows him on*)

Sir Provost. You will make arrangements to have this young monk sent back to England and taken to his convent, in Hastings, where his Abbot will keep him under supervision until my return. I want him treated without brutality, but very closely watched. I hold you personally responsible for him.

PROVOST. Very good, my Lord.

(*The* PROVOST *motions to the Soldiers.*

The SOLDIERS *surround the* MONK *and lead him off* R, *without a further glance from* BECKET. *Left alone,* BECKET *looks at the knife, smiles and wrinkles his nose*)

Becket (*in a murmur; with faint distaste*) It's touching, but it stinks all the same. (*He flings the knife away, and whistling his little march, goes to the tent, opens it and calls out lightheartedly*) Well, my prince, have you put on your Sunday best? It's time to go. We mustn't keep the Bishop waiting.

Becket *goes into the tent as—*

the Lights *dim to* Black-out

There is a sudden joyful peal of bells

Scene 2

Scene—*A Street in France.*

When the lights come up, Soldiers *enter up* l *and hang flags on two or more of the pillars. Then* Becket *enters up* l, *on foot, leading the* King *on horseback. They are followed by the four* Barons, *also mounted. The procession comes through the pillars. Acclamations from the crowd, bells and trumpets are heard off.*

King (*beaming as he waves*) Listen to that! They adore us, these French.

(*The sounds off quieten*)

Becket. It cost me quite a bit. I had money distributed among the populace this morning. The prosperous classes are at home, sulking, of course.

King. Patriots?

Becket. No. But they would have cost too much. There are also a certain number of your Highness's soldiers among the crowd, in disguise, to encourage any lukewarm elements.

King. Why do you always make a game of destroying my illusions? I thought they loved me for myself. You're an amoral man, Becket. (*Anxiously*) Does one say amoral or immoral?

Becket (*smiling*) It depends what one means.

King (*pointing*) She's pretty, look—the girl on the balcony, to the right there. Suppose we stopped a minute . . .

Becket. Impossible. The Bishop is waiting in the cathedral.

King. It would be a lot more fun than going to see a bishop.

Becket. My Lord, do you remember what you have to say to him?

King (*waving to the crowd*) Yes, yes, yes! As if it mattered what I say to a French bishop, whose city I've just taken by force.

Becket. It matters a great deal. For our future policy.

King. Am I the strongest or am I not?

BECKET. You are, today. But one must never drive one's enemy to despair. It makes him strong. A good occupational force must not crush, it must corrupt.

KING (*waving graciously*) What about my pleasure, then? Where does that enter into your scheme of things? Suppose I charged into this heap of frog-eaters now instead of acting the goat at their *Te Deum*? I can indulge in a bit of pleasure, can't I? I'm the conqueror.

BECKET. That would be a fault. Worse, a failing. One can permit oneself anything, Sir, but one must never indulge.

KING. Yes, Papa, right, Papa. What a bore you are today. (*He points*) Look at that little redhead there, standing on the fountain. Give orders for the procession to follow the same route back.

> The KING *exits down* L, *turning on his horse to watch the Girl out of sight.*

> BECKET *and the* BARONS *follow him off as—*

> *the* LIGHTS *dim to* BLACK-OUT

> *Organ music is heard*

SCENE 3

SCENE—*The Sacristy of a Cathedral in France.*

When the LIGHTS *come up, the sacristy is empty. The organ is heard, swelling chords. The organist is practising in the empty cathedral. The* KING, *attired for the ceremony, and the four* BARONS *enter down* L. *A* FRENCH PRIEST *and a* CHOIRBOY *follow them on. The* CHOIRBOY *carries a stool which he sets* RC *for the King. The* KING *sits impatiently on the stool. The* PRIEST *and* CHOIRBOY *stand together down* LC. *The* 1ST BARON *stands down* R. *The* 2ND BARON *is up* R *of the King, the* 3RD BARON *is up* L *of him and the* 4TH BARON *stands* C. *They seem to be waiting for something.*

KING. Where's Becket? And what are we waiting for?

> (*The organ music fades*)

1ST BARON. He just said to wait, my Lord. It seems there's something not quite in order.

KING (*ill-humouredly*) What a lot of fuss for a French Bishop. What do I look like, I ask you, hanging about in this sacristy like a village bridegroom?

4TH BARON (*moving to* L *of the King*) I quite agree, my Lord. I can't think why we don't march straight in. After all, it's your cathedral now. (*Eagerly*) Shall we just draw our swords and charge?

(*The other* Barons *react*)

King (*with a worried frown*) No. (*He rises*) Becket wouldn't like it. (*He resumes his seat*) If he told us to wait, there must be a good reason.

(Becket *enters hurriedly down* R *and crosses to* c)

Well, Becket, what's happening? We're freezing to death in here. What do these French think they're at, keeping us mouldering in this sacristy?

Becket. The order came from me, Sire. I'm having the cathedral evacuated.

(*The* King *rises. The* 2nd Baron *draws his sword. The other three follow suit*)

My police are certain that a French rising was to break out during the ceremony.

2nd Baron. God's blood! Shall we go in and deal with it, my Lord?

4th Baron. We'll make short work of it.

3rd Baron. Just say the word, Sire.

Becket (*curtly*) I forbid it. The King is quite safe in here, I've put guards on all the doors. Sheathe your swords.

(*The* Barons *sheathe their swords*)

(*He crosses down* R) No provocation, please. We are at the mercy of a chance incident and I still have no more than the forty men-at-arms in the city.

(*The* King *moves to* l *of Becket and tugs at his sleeve*)

King. Becket! Is that priest French?

Becket. Yes. But he is part of the Bishop's immediate entourage. And the Bishop is our man.

King. That man has a funny look in his eyes.

Becket. Who, the Bishop?

King. No. That priest.

(Becket *glances at the Priest and laughs*)

Becket. Of course, my prince, he squints. It would be tactless to ask him to leave. (*He turns to go*)

King. Becket!

Becket (*stopping and turning*) Sire?

King. The choirboy?

Becket (*laughing*) He's only so high.

King. He may be a dwarf. You never know with the French.

BECKET. I'll come straight back.

(BECKET *exits down* R. *The* KING *darts anxious looks on the* PRIEST *as he paces up and down muttering his prayers*)

KING. Baron!

(*The* 4TH BARON *moves to* L *of the King*)

4TH BARON (*bellowing*) My Lord?
KING. Shush! Keep an eye on that man, all four of you, and at the slightest move, leap on him.

(*The* BARONS *surround the Priest. The* CHOIRBOY *crosses towards the King. The* KING *shouts. The* BARONS *draw their swords and move towards the Boy. There is a sudden violent knocking off* R.
The BOY *screams, turns and runs off down* L)

(*He looks* R. *With a start*) What is it?

(*The* 1ST SOLDIER *enters down* R, *carrying a letter*)

1ST SOLDIER (*crossing and handing the letter to the 4th Baron*) An urgent letter from London, my Lord.

(*The* 4TH BARON *hands the letter to the King, who glances through it. The* SOLDIER *exits down* R)

KING. Good news, gentlemen. We have one enemy the less.

(BECKET *enters down* R)

(*Joyfully*) Becket!
BECKET. Everything is going according to plan, my prince. The rest of the troops are on their way.
KING (*cheerfully*) You're right, Becket, everything is going according to plan. God isn't angry with us. He has just recalled the Archbishop.
BECKET (*in a murmur*) That little old man. How could that feeble body contain so much strength?
KING. Now, now, now! Don't squander your sorrow, my son. I personally consider this an excellent piece of news. (*He hands the letter to the 4th Baron*)
BECKET. He was the first Norman who took an interest in me. He was a true father to me. God rest his soul.
KING. He will. After all the fellow did for Him, he's gone to Heaven, don't worry. Where he'll be infinitely more use to God than he was to us.

(*The* BARONS *move up* RC *and group together*)

(*He pulls Becket to him*) Becket! My little Becket, I think the ball's in our court, now. This is the time to score a point. (*He seizes Becket's arm, tense and quite transformed*) An extraordinary idea is

just creeping into my mind, Becket. A master-stroke. I can't think
what's got into me this morning, but I suddenly feel extremely
intelligent. It probably comes of making love with a French girl
last night. I am subtle, Becket, I am profound. So profound it's
making my head spin. Are you sure it isn't dangerous to think too
hard? Thomas, my little Thomas. Are you listening to me?

BECKET (*smiling at the King's excitement*) Yes, my prince.

KING (*as excited as a little boy*) Are you listening carefully?
Listen, Thomas. You told me once that the best ideas are the
stupidest, but the clever thing is to think of them. Listen, Thomas.
Tradition prevents me from touching the privileges of the Primacy. You follow me so far?

BECKET. Yes, my prince.

KING. But what if the Primate is my man? If the Archbishop
of Canterbury is for the King, how can his power possibly in-
commodate me?

BECKET. That's an ingenious idea, my prince, but you forget
that his election is a free one.

KING. No. You're forgetting the Royal Veto. It's fully a
hundred years since the Conclave of Bishops has voted contrary
to the wishes of the King.

BECKET. I don't doubt it, my Lord. But we know all your
Bishops. Which of them could you rely on? Once the Primate's
mitre is on their heads, they grow dizzy with power.

KING. Are you asking me, Becket? I'll tell you. Someone who
doesn't know what dizziness means. (*He circles to* C) Someone
who isn't even afraid of God. Thomas, my son, I'm sorry to
deprivate you of French girls and the fun of battle, but you are
going over to England.

BECKET. I am at your service, my prince.

KING. Can you guess what your mission will be?

(*A tremor of anguish crosses* BECKET's *face at what is to come*)

BECKET. No, my prince.

KING. You are going to deliver a personal letter from me to
every Bishop in the land. (*He moves to Becket*) And do you know
what those letters will contain, my Thomas, my little brother?
My royal wish to have you elected Primate of England.

(BECKET *is deathly white*)

BECKET (*with a forced laugh*) You're joking, of course, my Lord.
(*He opens his fine coat to display his even finer doublet*) Just look at the
edifying man, the saintly man whom you would be trusting with
these holy functions. Why, my prince—

(*The* KING *backs away* C, *clapping his hands*)

—you really fooled me for a second.

(*The* KING *bursts out laughing*)

(*He laughs, rather too loudly in his relief*) A fine Archbishop I'd have made. Look at my new shoes. They're the latest fashion in Paris. Attractive, that little upturned toe, don't you think? Quite full of unction and compunction, isn't it, Sire?

(*The* KING *suddenly stops laughing*)

KING. Shut up about your shoes, Thomas. I'm in deadly earnest. I shall write those letters before noon. You will help me.

(BECKET *is deathly pale*)

BECKET (*stammering*) But, my Lord, I'm not even a priest.
KING (*tersely*) You're a deacon. You can take your final vows on Monday and be ordained within a month.
BECKET. But have you considered what the Pope will say?
KING (*brutally*) I'll pay the price.
BECKET (*after an anguished pause*) My Lord, I see now that you weren't joking. Don't do this.
KING. Why not?
BECKET. It frightens me.
KING (*his face set and hard*) Becket, this is an order.

(*There is a pause.* BECKET *stands as if turned to stone*)

BECKET (*gravely*) If I become Archbishop, I can no longer be your friend.

(*An* OFFICER *enters down* R)

OFFICER (*to Becket*) The Church is now empty, my Lord. (*To the King*) The Bishop and his clergy await your Highness's good pleasure.
KING (*to Becket; roughly*) Did you hear that, Becket? Pull yourself together. You have an odd way of taking good news. Wake up! They say we can go in now.

(*The procession forms with the* PRIEST *leading.* BECKET *takes his place almost reluctantly a pace or so behind the* KING. *The* BARONS *form up behind Becket*)

BECKET (*in a murmur*) This is madness, my Lord. Don't do it. I could not serve both God and you.
KING (*looking straight ahead; stonily*) You've never disappointed me, Thomas. And you are the only man I trust. You will leave tonight.

The KING *motions to the Priest. The procession moves off down* R *as—*

the LIGHTS *dim to* BLACK-OUT

SCENE 4

SCENE—*A room in Becket's Palace.*

There is a large chest LC, *and a crucifix on one of the pillars.*

When the LIGHTS *come up, two* SERVANTS *are piling costly clothes into the chest. The* 2ND SERVANT *is the younger of the two.*

2ND SERVANT. The coat with the sable trimming, as well?

1ST SERVANT. Everything. You heard what he said.

2ND SERVANT (*grumbling*) Sables! To beggars! Who'll give them alms if they beg with that on their backs. They'll starve to death.

1ST SERVANT (*cackling*) They'll eat the sables. Can't you understand, you idiot. He's going to sell all this and give them the money.

2ND SERVANT. But what will he wear himself? He's got nothing left at all.

(BECKET *enters up* L. *He is wearing a plain grey dressing-gown*)

BECKET. Are the chests full? I want them sent over to the Jew before tonight. I want nothing left in this room but the bare walls. Gil, the fur coverlet.

1ST SERVANT (*regretfully*) My Lord will be cold at night.

BECKET. Do as I say.

(*The* 1ST SERVANT *regretfully takes the coverlet that was on the couch in Act I, Scene 6 and puts it in the chest*)

Has the steward been told about tonight's meal? Supper for forty in the great hall.

1ST SERVANT. Yes, my Lord.

2ND SERVANT. But the steward says could he have your list of invitations fairly soon, my Lord. He only has three runners and he's afraid there won't be time to . . .

BECKET. There are no invitations. The great doors will be thrown open and you will go out into the street and tell the poor they are dining with me tonight.

1ST SERVANT (*appalled*) Very good, my Lord.

(*The* SERVANTS *move towards the pillars, to go*)

BECKET. I want the service to be impeccable. The dishes presented to each guest first, with full ceremony, just as for princes. Go now.

(*The* SERVANTS *go through the pillars and exit up* R.)

(*He looks casually over one or two articles of clothing in the chest*) I must say it was all very pretty stuff. (*He drops the lid and bursts out laughing*) A prick of vanity. The mark of an upstart. A truly saintly man would never have done the whole thing in one day. Nobody will ever believe it's genuine. (*He turns to the crucifix on the pillar. Simply*) I hope You haven't inspired me with all these holy resolutions in order to make me look ridiculous, Lord? It's all so new to me. I'm setting about it a little clumsily perhaps. (*He looks at the crucifix and with a swift gesture takes it off the pillar*) And You're far too sumptuous, too. Precious stones around Your bleeding Body. I shall give You to some poor village church. (*He lays the crucifix on the chest, then looks around the room, happy and light-hearted*) It's like leaving for a holiday. Forgive me, Lord, but I never enjoyed myself so much in my whole life. I don't believe You are a sad God. The joy I feel in shedding all my riches must be part of Your divine intentions.

(BECKET *goes behind the tapestry up* LC, *where he can be heard gaily whistling his marching song. He comes back a few seconds later, his bare feet in sandals and wearing a monk's coarse woollen robe*)

(*He moves to the chest*) There. Farewell, Becket. I wish there had been something I regretted parting with, so I could offer it to You. (*He picks up the crucifix and looks at it. Simply*) Lord, are You sure You are not tempting me? It all seems far too easy.

BECKET *drops to his knees and prays as—*

the CURTAIN *falls*

ACT III

Scene i

SCENE—*A room in the King's Palace.*

The pillars are backed by tapestries. There is a bench down R, *and an armchair* RC. *The brazier is down* C.

When the CURTAIN *rises, the* QUEEN MOTHER *is seated* RC. *The* YOUNG QUEEN *is seated on the bench down* R. *They are working at their tapestry. The* PRINCES, *the King's two sons, are playing cats' cradles on the floor down* LC. *One of them is considerably older than the other. The* KING, *whistling to himself, is standing between the pillars playing at cup-and-ball. After several unsuccessful attempts to catch the ball in the cup, he moves to* L *of the Queen Mother.*

KING (*irritably*) Forty beggars! He invited forty beggars to dinner.

QUEEN MOTHER. The dramatic gesture, as usual. I always said you had misplaced your confidence, my son.

KING (*pacing to* LC) Madam, I am very particular where I place my confidence. (*He tosses the cup-and-ball to the younger Prince*)

(*The elder* PRINCE *sulks*)

I only ever did it once in my whole life and I am still convinced I was right. (*He moves to the pillars*)

YOUNG QUEEN. It seems he has sold his gold plate and all his rich clothes to a Jew. He wears an ordinary homespun habit, now.

(*The* KING *moves down* C)

QUEEN MOTHER. I see that as a sign of ostentation, if nothing worse. One can become a saint, certainly, but not in a single day. I've never liked the man. You were insane to make him so powerful.

KING (*crying out*) He is my friend.

QUEEN MOTHER (*acidly*) More's the pity.

YOUNG QUEEN. He is your friend in debauchery. It was he who lured you away from your duty towards me. It was he who first took you to the whorehouses.

KING (*moving towards the Young Queen; furiously*) Rubbish, Madam! I didn't need anybody to lure me away from my duty towards you. I made you three children, very conscientiously.

43

Phew! My duty is done for a while. To be perfectly frank, you
bore me. You and your eternal backbiting, over your everlasting tapestry, the pair of you. That's no sustenance for a man.
(*He paces furiously* LC, *then back to* RC) If at least it had some
artistic merit. My ancestress Mathilda, *she* embroidered a master-
piece—which they left behind in Bayeux, more's the pity. (*He
points to the Young Queen's tapestry*) But that! It's beyond belief
it's so mediocre.

  YOUNG QUEEN (*nettled*) We can only use the gifts we're born
with.

  KING. Yes. And yours are meagre. (*He crosses to* C. *With a sigh*)
I've been bored to tears for a whole month. Not a soul to talk to.
(*He moves between the pillars*) After his nomination, not wanting to
seem in too indecent a hurry, I leave him alone to carry out his
pastoral tour. Now, back he comes at last, I summon him to the
palace and he's late! (*He turns and looks off up* R) Ah! Someone at
the sentry post. (*He turns, disappointed*) No, it's only a monk. (*He
wanders aimlessly* LC *and watches the Princes playing. Sourly*) Charming babes. Men in the making. Sly and obtuse already. And to
think one is expected to be dewy-eyed over creatures like that.
(*To the Princes*) Which is the elder of you two?

  ELDER PRINCE (*rising*) I am, Sir.

  KING. What's your name again?

  ELDER PRINCE. Henry the Third.

  KING (*sharply*) Not yet, Sir. Number Two is in the best of
health.

  (*The Elder Prince sits on the floor*)

(*He moves* RC. *To the Young Queen*) You've brought them up well.
Do you think of yourself as Regent already? And you wonder
that I shun your bedchamber? I don't care to make love with my
widow.

  (*An* OFFICER *enters between the pillars*)

  OFFICER. A messenger from the Archbishop, my Lord.

  KING (*beside himself with rage*) A messenger! A messenger! I
summoned the Archbishop Primate in person and he sends me a
messenger! (*He turns to the Queens, suddenly uneasy, almost touching*)
Perhaps he's ill? That would explain everything.

  QUEEN MOTHER (*bitterly*) That would be too much to hope
for.

  KING (*raging*) You'd like to see him dead, wouldn't you, you
females—because he loves me? If he hasn't come, it's because he's
dying. (*He moves to the Officer*) Send the man in, quickly. Oh, my
Thomas . . .

(*The* Officer *exits between the pillars and re-enters almost immediately.*

Etienne, *a monk, follows him on*)

(*To Etienne*) Is Becket ill?

Etienne (*falling on one knee*) Sire?

(*The* Officer *exits between the pillars*)

King. Is your master ill?
Etienne. His Grace is in good health. He has charged me to deliver this letter with his deepest respects—and to give your Highness this. (*He hands a parchment and the Seal to the King*)
King (*stunned*) The Seal? (*He crosses to* l *of the Queen Mother*) Why has he sent me back the Seal? (*He unrolls the parchment and reads it in silence. His face hardens. Curtly, without looking at Etienne*) Go.

(Etienne *rises*)

Etienne. Is there an answer from your Highness for His Grace the Archbishop?
King. No.

(Etienne *exits between the pillars. The* King *stands still a moment, at a loss, glowering. The* Queens *exchange a conspiratorial look*)

Queen Mother (*rising and moving to the King; insidiously*) Well, my son, what does your friend say in his letter?
King (*bawling*) Get out! Get out, both of you. And take your royal vermin with you.

(*The* Young Queen *and the* Princes *rise and exit hurriedly between the pillars.*
The Queen Mother *follows them off*)

(*He stands a moment, reeling a little as if stunned by the blow, then he moves to the bench down* r *and collapses on it, moaning*) I am alone! Oh, my Thomas! (*He remains a moment prostrate, then collects himself and sits up. He looks at the Seal in his hand. Between clenched teeth*) You've sent me back the three Lions of England, like a little boy who doesn't want to play with me any more. You think you have God's Honour to defend now. I would have gone to war with all England's might behind me, and against England's interests to defend you, little Saxon. I would have given the honour of the Kingdom laughingly—for you. Only I loved you and you didn't love me—that's the difference. (*His face hardens. Between clenched teeth*) Thanks all the same for this last gift as you desert me. I shall learn to be alone.

The Lights *dim to* Black-out

SCENE 2

SCENE—*The Episcopal Palace.*

When the LIGHTS *come up, an* ENGLISH PRIEST *enters up* RC, *showing in two* MONKS *and the* YOUNG MONK *from Hastings.*

PRIEST. His Grace will receive you here. (*He stands up* R)

(*The two* MONKS *are impressed. They push the* YOUNG MONK *about a little*)

1ST MONK. Stand up straight. Kiss his Grace's ring and try to answer his questions with humility, or I'll tan your backside for you.

2ND MONK. I suppose you thought he'd forgotten all about you? Well, don't you act proud with him or you'll be sorry.

(BECKET *enters down* L *and crosses to the Monks. He wears a monk's coarse robe*)

BECKET. Well, brothers, is it fine over in Hastings? (*He holds out his ringed hand*)

(*The three* MONKS *in turn kiss the ring*)

1ST MONK. Foggy, my Lord.

BECKET (*smiling*) Then it's fine in Hastings. (*He moves* C) How has this young man been behaving? Has he given our Abbot much trouble?

2ND MONK. A proper mule, my Lord. The stubborn little wretch is just the same; all defiance and insults. He has fallen into the sin of pride. Nothing I know of will pull him out of that.

1ST MONK. Save a good kick in the rump, perhaps—if Your Grace will pardon the expression. (*To the Young Monk*) Stand up straight.

BECKET (*to the Young Monk*) Pay attention to your brother. Stand up straight. As a rule the sin of pride stiffens a man's back. Look me in the face.

(*The* YOUNG MONK *looks at Becket*)

Good. (*He looks at the Young Monk for a while, then turns to the others*) Well, brothers, refresh yourselves in the kitchen before you leave. Don't spurn our hospitality; we relieve you, for today, of your vows of abstinence, and we fondly hope you will do honour to our bill of fare. Greet our father Abbot in Jesus on our behalf.

2ND MONK (*hesitantly*) And the lad?

BECKET. We will keep him here with us.

1st Monk. Watch out for him, your Grace. He's vicious.

Becket (*smiling*) We are not afraid.

(*The two* Monks *each down* R. Becket *and the* Young Monk *remain, facing each other*)

Why do you hold yourself so badly?

Young Monk. Because I can't look people in the face any more.

Becket. I'll teach you. Look at me.

(*The* Young Monk *gives Becket a sidelong glance*)

Better than that.

(*The* Young Monk *looks at Becket*)

Are you still bearing the full weight of England's shame on your back?

Young Monk. Yes.

Becket. If I took over half of it, would it weigh less heavy? (*He motions to the Priest*) Show in their Lordships.

(*The* Priest *exits between the pillars*)

(*Confidentially, with a smile*) It is time for my Council with their Lordships the Bishops. You'll soon see that being alone is not a privilege reserved entirely for you.

(*The* Bishop of Oxford, *the* Bishop of York, *and* Folliot *enter between the pillars*)

(*He leads the Young Monk down* R) You stay here in the corner. I ask only one thing. Don't leap at their throats; you'd complicate everything. (*He turns and moves* LC)

Folliot (*moving to* R *of Becket*) Your Grace, I am afraid this meeting may be a pointless one. You insisted—against our advice, on attacking the King openly. But even before the excommunications which you asked us to sanction could be made public, the King has hit back. His Grand Justicer has just arrived in your ante-chamber and is demanding to see you. He is the bearer of an official order summoning you to appear before his assembled Council within twenty-four hours and there to answer the charges made against you.

Becket. Of what is the King accusing me?

Folliot. Prevarication. His Highness demands a considerable sum of money still outstanding on your administration of the Treasury.

(*The other two* Bishops *move to* R *of Folliot*)

Becket. When I resigned the Chancellorship I handed over

my ledgers to his Grand Justicer, who acquitted me of all sub-
sequent dues and claims. What does the King demand?

BISHOP OF OXFORD. Forty thousand marks in fine gold.

BECKET (*smiling*) I don't believe there was ever that much gold
in all the coffers of all England in all the time I was Chancellor.
But a clever clerk can soon change that. (*He smiles and looks at
them*) I have the impression, gentlemen, that you must be feeling
something very akin to relief.

BISHOP OF YORK. We advised you against open opposition. You
insisted on these excommunications.

BECKET. William of Aynsford struck down the priest I had
appointed to a parish on his domains, on the pretext that the
King disapproved of my choice. Am I to look on while my
priests are murdered?

BISHOP OF OXFORD (*quietly*) This excommunication was bad
policy, your Grace. William of Aynsford is a companion of the
King.

BISHOP OF YORK (*yelping*) And his wife is my second cousin.

BECKET. That is a detail I deplore, my Lord Bishop, but he
has killed one of my priests. If I do not defend my priests, who
will? Gilbert of Clare has indicted before his lay Court of Justice
a churchman who was under our exclusive jurisdiction.

BISHOP OF YORK. An interesting victim, I must say. The man
was accused of rape and murder. Wouldn't it have been cleverer
to let the wretch hang—and have peace?

BECKET. "I bring not peace but the sword." Your Lordship
must surely have read that somewhere. If I allow my priests to be
tried by a secular tribunal, I don't give much for our chances of
survival in five years' time, my Lord. I have excommunicated
Gilbert of Clare, and William of Aynsford. The Kingdom of God
must be defended like any other Kingdom. You passed the burden
on to me and now I have to carry it, and nothing will ever make
me set it down again. I thank your Lordships. The Council is
adjourned. I shall stand by these excommunications. And I shall
appear tomorrow before the King's High Court of Justice.

(*The* BISHOPS *and* PRIEST *look at one another in surprise, then bow
and exit through the pillars*)

(*He turns to the Young Monk*) Well, does shame weigh less heavy
now? (*He moves to him*)

YOUNG MONK. Yes.

BECKET (*putting an arm around the Young Monk*) Then stand up
straight.

BECKET, *laughing, leads the* YOUNG MONK *off down* R *as—*

the LIGHTS *dim to* BLACK-OUT

SCENE 3

SCENE—*A room in the King's Palace.*

    The setting is the same as Act III, Scene 1.

When the LIGHTS *come up, the armchair is* RC. *The* KING *is pacing up and down, clearly waiting for someone. The sound of distant trumpets is heard. The* KING *moves to the chair and sits.* FOLLIOT *enters hurriedly down* L.

KING. What's happening?

FOLLIOT. Legal procedure is taking its course, your Highness. The third summons has been delivered. Becket has not appeared. (*He crosses to* L *of the King*) In a moment he will be condemned *in absentia.* I shall then, as Bishop of London, step forward and publicly accuse Becket of having celebrated, in contempt of the King, a sacrilegious Mass at the instigation of the Evil Spirit.

KING (*anxiously*) Isn't that going rather far?

FOLLIOT. Of course. It won't fool anyone, but it always works. The assembly will then go out to vote and return a verdict of imprisonment. The sentence is already drawn up.

KING. Unanimously?

FOLLIOT. We are all Normans. The rest is your Highness's concern. It will merely be a matter of carrying out the sentence. (*He crosses to* L.)

KING (*staggering suddenly*) Oh, my Thomas!

FOLLIOT (*impassively*) I can still stop the machine, your Highness.

KING (*after a moment's hesitation*) No. Go.

    (FOLLIOT *exits down* L.

      The QUEEN MOTHER *and the* YOUNG QUEEN *enter through the pillars. The* KING *rises and moves* C. *There is a pause*)

YOUNG QUEEN (*moving to* R *of the* KING) He's doomed, isn't he?

KING (*dully*) Yes.

YOUNG QUEEN. At last!

    (*The* KING *turns on the Young Queen, his face twisted with hate*)

KING. I forbid you to gloat.

YOUNG QUEEN. At seeing your enemy perish—why not?

KING (*frothing*) Becket is my enemy. I am forced to fight him and to crush him, but at least he gave me, with open hands, everything that is at all good in me.

    (*The* QUEEN MOTHER *moves down* LC)

And you have never given me anything but your carping mediocrity, your everlasting obsession with your puny little perso͏r. ᴀnd what you thought was due to it. That is why I forbid you to smile as he lies dying.

Young Queen. I gave you my youth. I gave you your children.

King (*shouting*) I don't like my children. And as for your youth—that dusty flower pressed in a hymn book since you were twelve years old, you can say farewell to that without a tear. Your body was an empty desert, Madam—which duty forced me to wander in alone. You have never been a wife to me.

(*The* Young Queen *moves* R)

And Becket was my friend, red-blooded—(*he crosses down* L) generous and full of strength. (*He is shaken by a sob*) Oh, my Thomas!

Queen Mother (*haughtily*) And I, my son, I gave you nothing, either, I suppose?

(*The* King *recovers his composure, moves to* L *of the Queen Mother and glares at her*)

King (*dully*) Life. Yes. Thank you. But after that I never saw you save in a passage, ten minutes before official ceremonies. I have always been alone, and no one on this earth has ever loved me except Becket.

Queen Mother (*bitterly*) Well, call him back. Absolve him, since he loves you. But do something.

King. I am. I'm learning to be alone again, Madam. As usual.

(*A* Page *enters breathlessly down* L)

(*He moves to the Page, grabs him and pulls him* C) Well? What's happening? How far have they got?

Page. My Liege, Thomas Becket appeared just when everyone had given him up; sick, deathly pale, in full pontifical regalia and carrying his own heavy silver cross. He walked the whole length of the hall without anyone daring to stop him, and when Robert Duke of Leicester began to read out his sentence, he stopped him with a gesture and forbade him, in God's name to pronounce judgement against him, his spiritual Father. Then he walked back through the crowd, which parted for him in silence. He has just left.

King (*unable to hide his delight*) Well played, Thomas! (*He checks himself, embarrassed*) And what about my Barons?

Page. Their hands flew to their swords crying "Traitor!" "Perjurer!" "Arrest him!" But not one of them dared move.

King (*with a roar*) The fools! I am surrounded by fools and the only intelligent man in my Kingdom is against me.

Page (*continuing his story*) Then, on the threshold, he turned, looked at them coldly as they stormed and shouted, and he said that not so long ago he could have answered their challenge sword in hand.

KING (*jubilantly*) He could beat them all! All, I tell you! On horseback, on foot, with a mace, with a lance, with a sword. In the lists they fell to him like ninepins.

PAGE. His eyes were so cold, and so ironic—that one by one, they fell silent. Only then did he turn and go out.

KING (*sombrely*) And what about the Bishop of London, who was going to reduce him to powder? What about my busy friend, Gilbert Folliot?

PAGE. He had a horrible fit of rage trying to incite the crowd, he let out a screech of foul abuse, and then he fainted. They are bringing him round now.

(*The* KING *suddenly bursts into a shout of irrepressible laughter and, watched by the two outraged* QUEENS, *collapses into the armchair* RC, *breathless and helpless with mirth*)

KING. It's too funny! It's too funny!

QUEEN MOTHER (*coldly*) You will laugh less heartily tomorrow, my son. If you don't stop him, Becket will reach the coast tonight, ask asylum of the King of France and jeer at you, unpunished, from across the Channel.

The QUEEN MOTHER *turns and sweeps out between the pillars.*
The YOUNG QUEEN *follows her off. The* KING *suddenly stops laughing and gazes out front as—*

the LIGHTS *dim to* BLACK-OUT

SCENE 4

SCENE—*The Court of Louis, King of France.*

There is a throne RC. *Banners are hanging up* RC.

When the LIGHTS *come up,* KING LOUIS *is seated very erect on the throne* RC. *He is a burly man with intelligent eyes. Two French* BARONS *are with him. The* 1ST BARON *stands* R *of the throne, the* 2ND BARON *is* L *of it. A* PAGE *sits at* LOUIS's *feet.*

LOUIS. Gentlemen, we are in France so phut to the King of England—

1ST BARON. Sire!

LOUIS. —as the old song goes.

1ST BARON. Your Majesty cannot *not* receive his Ambassadors extraordinary.

LOUIS. Ordinary, or extraordinary, I am at home to all ambassadors. It's my job. I shall receive them.

1st Baron. They have been waiting in your Majesty's ante-room for over an hour, Sire.

Louis. Let them wait. That's *their* job. I know what they are going to ask me.

2nd Baron. The extradition of a felon is a courtesy due from one crowned head to another.

Louis. My dear man, crowned heads can play the little game of courtesy, but nations owe each other none. My right to play the courteous gentleman stops where France's interests begin. And France's interests consist in making things as difficult as possible for England—a thing England never hesitates to do for us. The Archbishop is a millstone round Henry Plantagenet's neck. Long live the Archbishop! Anyway, I like the fellow. Remember our last peace treaty with Henry when he guaranteed to spare the lives of the refugees in Brittany. Two months later all of them had lost their heads. That directly touched my personal honour. I was not strong enough at the time, so I had to pretend I hadn't heard of these men's execution. And I continued to lavish smiles on my English cousin. But praise God our affairs have taken a turn for the better. And today *he* needs *us*. So I will now proceed to remember my honour. Show in the ambassadors.

(*The* 1st Baron *exits between the pillars up* L. *The* Page *rises and stands up* L *of the throne.*
The 1st Baron *re-enters and crosses to* c.
Folliot *and the* Duke of Arundel *follow him on.* Folliot *carries a parchment*)

1st Baron. Permit me to introduce to your Majesty the two envoys extraordinary from his Highness Henry of England—the Duke of Arundel and His Grace the Bishop of London.

(Arundel *and* Folliot *go down on one knee*)

Louis (*with a friendly wave to Arundel*) Greetings to you, Milord. I have not forgotten your amazing exploits at the last tournament at Calais. Do you still wield a lance as mightily as you did, milord?

Arundel (*rising and making a gratified bow*) I hope so, Sire.

(Folliot *rises and unrolls his parchment*)

Louis. Bishop, I see you have a letter for us from your master. We are listening.

(Folliot *bows*)

Folliot (*reading*) "To my Lord and friend, Louis, King of the French, from Henry, King of England, Duke of Normandy, Duke of Aquitaine and Count of Anjou. Learn that Thomas, former Archbishop of Canterbury, has been found guilty of fraud, perjury and treason towards me. He has forthwith fled my kingdom as a traitor, and with evil intent. I therefore entreat you not to allow this criminal to reside upon your territories, not to permit any of your vassals to give help, support or counsel to this my greatest enemy. I expect you to assist me in the vindication of my honour as you would wish me to do for you, should the need arise."

(*There is a pause.* FOLLIOT *bows very low and holds the parchment out to* LOUIS, *who ignores it*)

LOUIS. We have listened attentively to our gracious cousin's request and we take good note of it. Our chancellery will draft a reply which will be sent to you tomorrow. All we can do at the moment is express our surprise. No news has reached us of the presence of the Archbishop of Canterbury on our domains.

FOLLIOT (*tersely*) Sire, the former Archbishop has taken refuge at the Abbey of St Martin, near St Omer.

LOUIS (*still gracious*) My Lord Bishop, we flatter ourselves that there is some order in our kingdom. If he were there, we would certainly have been informed. (*He makes a gesture of dismissal*)

(FOLLIOT *and* ARUNDEL *bow, and exit backwards through the pillars up* L, *ushered out by the* 1ST BARON)

(*To the* 2ND BARON) Show in Thomas Becket and leave us.

(*The* 2ND BARON *exits down* R. LOUIS *dismisses the Page.*
The PAGE *exits up* R.
The 2ND BARON *ushers* BECKET *in down* R. BECKET *is wearing his monk's robe.*
The 2ND BARON *exits down* R. BECKET *goes to drop on to one knee*)

(*Kindly*) Rise, Thomas Becket, and greet us as the Primate of England. The bow is enough—and if I know my etiquette—you are entitled to a slight nod of the head from me.

(BECKET *bows*)

(*He nods*) There, that's done. I would even be required to kiss your ring, if your visit were an official one. But I have the impression that it isn't—am I right?

BECKET (*with a smile*) No, Sire. I am only an exile.

LOUIS (*graciously*) That, too, is an important title in France.

BECKET. I am afraid it is the only one I have left. My property has been seized and distributed to those who served the King against me. John, Bishop of Poitiers, who was suspected of wanting to grant me asylum, has just been poisoned.

LOUIS (*smiling*) In fact, you are a very dangerous man.

BECKET. I'm afraid so.

LOUIS (*unperturbed*) We like danger, Becket. And if the King of France started being afraid of the King of England, there would be something sadly amiss in Europe. We grant you our royal protection on whichever of our domains it will please you to choose.

BECKET. I humbly thank your Majesty. I must, however, tell you that I cannot buy this protection with any act hostile to my country.

LOUIS. You do us injury. That was understood. You may be sure we are practised enough in the task of kingship not to make such gross errors in our choice of spies and traitors. The King of France will ask nothing of you. But . . . (*He rises heavily on to his fat legs*) There is always a but, as I'm sure you are aware, in politics.

(BECKET *looks up*)

I am only responsible for France's interests, Becket. (*He moves* R) I really can't afford to shoulder those of Heaven.

(BECKET *moves to* L *of Louis*)

In a month or a year I can summon you back here and tell you, just as blandly, that my dealings with the King of England have taken a different turn and that I am obliged to banish you. (*He slaps Becket affably on the back, his eyes sparkling with intelligence. With a smile*) I believe you have dabbled in politics, too, Archbishop.

BECKET (*smiling*) Yes, Sire. Not so very long ago.

LOUIS (*jovially*) I like you very much. Mark you, had you been a French Bishop, I don't say I wouldn't have clapped you into prison myself. But in the present circumstances, you have a right to my royal protection. Do you value candour, Becket?

BECKET. Yes, Sire.

LOUIS. Then we are sure to understand each other. Do you intend to visit the Holy Father?

BECKET. Yes, Sire, if you give me your safe conduct.

LOUIS. You shall have it. But a word in your ear—as a friend. (*He puts his hand on Becket's shoulder*) Keep this to yourself, won't you? Don't go and stir up trouble for me with Rome. Beware the Pope. He'll sell you for thirty pieces of silver.

(*There is a slight interjection from* BECKET)

The man needs money.

The LIGHTS *dim to* BLACK-OUT

Scene 5

Scene—*The Pope's Palace in Rome.*

There are two gilt throne-chairs c.

When the Lights *come up, the* Pope *and a* Cardinal *are seated* c. *The* Pope *is a thin, fidgety little man with an atrocious Italian accent. The* Cardinal *is swarthy, and his accent is even worse. The whole effect is a little grubby, among the gilded splendour.*

Pope. I don't agree, Zambelli. I don't agree at all. It's a very bad plan altogether. We will forfeit our honour all for three thousand silver marks.

Cardinal. Holy Father, there is no question of forfeiting honour, but merely of taking the sum offered by the King of England and thereby gaining time.

Pope (*concerned*) If we take the money from the King, I cannot possibly receive the Archbishop.

Cardinal. Receive the money from the King, Very Holy Father, and receive the Archbishop, too. The one will neutralize the other.

Pope (*gloomily*) I don't want to receive him at all. I gather he is a sincere man. I am always disconcerted by people of that sort. They leave me with a bad taste in my mouth.

Cardinal. Sincerity is a form of strategy, just like any other, Holy Father. In certain very difficult negotiations, when the usual tactics cease to work, I have been known to use it myself. The great pitfall, of course is if your opponent starts being sincere at the same time as you. Then the game becomes horribly confusing.

Pope. You know what they say Becket's been meaning to ask me, do you—in the month he's spent pacing about my antechamber?

Cardinal (*innocently*) No, Holy Father.

Pope (*impatiently*) Zambelli! Don't play the fox with me! It was you who told me.

Cardinal (*caught out*) I beg your pardon, Holy Father, I had forgotten. Or rather, as your Holiness asked me the question, I thought you had forgotten and so I took a chance and . . .

Pope (*irritably*) Zambelli, if we start outmanoeuvring each other to no purpose, we'll be here all night.

Cardinal (*in confusion*) Force of habit, your Holiness. Excuse me.

Pope. Becket means to ask me to relieve him of his rank and functions as Archbishop of Canterbury—that's the reason Becket is in Rome. And do you know why he wants to ask me that?

Cardinal (*candidly for once*) Yes, Holy Father.

Pope. No, you do not know. It was your enemy Rapallo who told me.

Cardinal (*modestly*) I know it just the same, because I have a spy in Rapallo's palace.

Pope (*with a wink*) Culograti?

Cardinal. No. Culograti is only my spy in his master's eyes. I have another man spying on Culograti.

Pope (*cutting short the digression*) Becket maintains that he owes his election to the Primacy solely to the royal whim and that consequently to the Honour of God, of which he has now decided he is the champion, does not allow him to bear this usurped title any longer. He wishes to be nothing more than an ordinary priest.

Cardinal (*after a moment's thought*) The man is clearly an abyss of ambition.

Pope. And yet he knows that we know that his title and functions are his only safeguard against the King's anger. I don't give much for his skin, wherever he is, when he is no longer Archbishop.

Cardinal (*thoughtfully*) He's playing a deep game. But I have a plan. Your Holiness will pretend to believe in his scruples. You will receive him and relieve him of his titles and functions as Primate, then, immediately after, as a reward for his zeal in defending the Church in England, you will reappoint him Archbishop, in right and due form this time. We thus avert the danger, we score a point against him—and at the same time a point against the King of England.

Pope. The King! That's a dangerous game. The King has a long arm.

Cardinal. We can cover ourselves. We will send secret letters to the English Court explaining that this new nomination is a pure formality. On the other hand, we will inform Becket of the existence of these secret letters, swearing him to secrecy and begging him to consider them as null and void.

Pope (*getting muddled*) In that case, perhaps there isn't much point in the letters being secret?

Cardinal. Yes, there is. Because that will allow us to man-oeuvre with each of them as if the other was ignorant of the contents, while taking the precaution of making it known to them both. The main thing is for them not to know that we know they know. It's so simple a child of twelve could grasp it.

Pope. But Archbishop or no—what are we going to do with Becket?

Cardinal (*with a lighthearted wave of the hand*) We will send him to a convent. A French convent, since King Louis is protect-ing him—to the Cistercians say, at Pontigny. The monastic rule is a strict one. It will do that one-time dandy a world of good. Let him learn real poverty. That will teach him to be the comforter of the poor.

POPE. That sounds like good advice, Zambelli.

CARDINAL. Thank you, Your Holiness.

POPE. Bread and water and nocturnal prayers are an excellent remedy for sincerity. (*He muses a moment*) The only thing that puzzles me, Zambelli, is why you should want to give me a piece of good advice.

The CARDINAL *looks a little embarrassed as—*

the LIGHTS *dim to* BLACK-OUT

SCENE 6

SCENE—*A Convent Cell.*

A humble wooden crucifix hangs on one of the pillars.
When the LIGHTS *come up,* BECKET *is on his knees, praying.*
The LITTLE MONK *is crouching on the floor* L, *carving a small wooden cross.*

BECKET. Yet, it would be simple enough. Too simple, perhaps. Sanctity is a temptation, too. Oh, how difficult it is to get an answer from You, Lord. I was slow in praying to You, but I cannot believe that others, worthier than myself, who have spent years asking You questions, have been better than I am at deciphering Your real intentions. I am only a beginner and I must make mistake after mistake, as I did in my Latin translations as a boy, when my riotous imagination made the old priest roar with laughter. But I cannot believe that one learns Your language as one learns any human tongue, by hard study, with a dictionary, a grammar and a set of idioms. I am sure, that to the hardened sinner, who drops to his knees for the first time and murmurs Your name, marvelling, You tell all Your secrets, straight away, and that he understands. I have served You like a dilettante, surprised that I could still find pleasure in that service. And for a long time I was on my guard because of it. I could not believe this pleasure would bring me one step nearer You. I could not believe that the road could be a happy one. The hair-shirts, the fasting, the bells in the small hours summoning one to meet You, on the icy paving-stones, in the sick misery of the poor ill-treated human animal—I cannot believe that all these are anything but safeguards for the weak. In power and in luxury, and even in the pleasures of the flesh, I shall not cease to speak to You, I feel this now. You are the God of the rich man and the happy man, too, Lord, and You do not turn away Your eyes from the man who was given everything from birth. And he may be Your true lost sheep. For Your Scheme of Things, which we mistakenly call Justice, is secret and profound and You plumb the hidden depths of poor men's puny frames as carefully as those of Kings. And beneath those outward differences, which blind us, but which to You are barely noticeable; beneath the diadem or the grime, You discern the same pride, the same vanity, the same petty, complacent preoccupation with oneself. Lord, I am certain now that You meant to tempt me with this hair-shirt, object of so much vapid self-congratulation; this bare cell, this solitude, this absurdly endured winter cold—and the conveniences of prayer. It would be too easy to buy You like this, at so low a price. I shall leave this convent, where so many precautions hem You round. I shall take up the Mitre and the golden Cope again, and the great silver cross and I shall go back and fight in the place and with the weapons it has pleased You to give me. It has pleased You to make me Archbishop and to set me, like a solitary pawn, face to face with the King, upon the chessboard. I shall go back to my place, humbly, and let the world accuse me of pride so that I may do what I believe is my life's work. For the rest, Your will be done. (*He crosses himself*)

   The LITTLE MONK *suddenly throws his knife into the floor at his feet and watches it as it quivers.*

CURTAIN

ACT IV

Scene i

SCENE—*The Court of King Louis.*

When the CURTAIN *rises,* LOUIS *is seated on his throne* RC, *reading a letter. The* 1ST BARON *is standing* L *of the throne. After a moment* LOUIS *looks up and nods to the* 1ST BARON *who exits* L. *There is a brief pause, then* BECKET *enters* L, *crosses to* C *and bows to* LOUIS. LOUIS *nods.*

LOUIS. I tell you, Becket, intrigue is an ugly thing. You keep the smell about you for ages afterwards. There is a return of good understanding between the Kingdom of England and ourselves. I must protect my rear by a truce with Henry Plantagenet before I march, as I must—against the Roman Emperor. And needless to say, you are one of the items on Henry's bill of charges. I can even tell you, that apart from yourself, his demands are negligible. (*Musingly*) Curious man. England's best policy would have been to take advantage of the Emperor's aggressive intentions and join forces with him. He is deliberately sacrificing this opportunity for the pleasure of seeing you driven out. He really hates you, doesn't he?

BECKET (*simply*) Sire, we loved each other and I think he cannot forgive me for preferring God to him.

LOUIS. Your King isn't doing his job properly, Archbishop. He is giving way to a passion. However. You are on his bill; I have to pay his price and banish you. I do not do so without a certain shame. Where are you thinking of going?

BECKET. I am a shepherd who has remained too long away from his flock. I intend to go back to England. I had already made my decision before this audience with your Majesty.

LOUIS (*surprised*) You have a taste for martyrdom? You disappoint me. I thought you more healthy-minded.

BECKET. Would it be healthy-minded to walk the roads of Europe, and beg a refuge where my carcass would be safe? Besides, where would I be safe? I am Primate of England. That is a rather showy label on my back. The honour of God and common sense, which for once coincide, dictate that I should go and have myself killed—if killed I must be—among my flock in my own cathedral. That is my place.

LOUIS (*after a pause*) I dare say you're right. (*He sighs*) Ah, what a pity it is to be a king, sometimes, when one has the surprise of meeting a man. You'll tell me, fortunately for me, that

59

men are rare. Why weren't you born on this side of the Channel, Becket? (*He smiles*) True, you'd have been a thorn in *my* side, then. The honour of God is a very cumbersome thing. (*He muses for a moment, then rises. Abruptly*) Who cares? I'll risk it. I like you too much. I'll indulge in a moment's humanity. I am meeting Henry in a day or two, at La Ferte Bernard, to seal our agreement. I shall try to persuade him to make his peace with you. Should he agree, will you be willing to talk with him?

BECKET. Sire, ever since we stopped seeing each other, I have never ceased to talk to him.

The LIGHTS *dim to* BLACK-OUT

SCENE 2

SCENE—*The plain of La Ferte Bernard.*

The set is completely empty. Nothing remains but the cyclorama around the bare stage. A vast, arid plain, lashed by the wind.

When the LIGHTS *come up, trumpets are heard. Two* SENTRIES *are standing down* R, *watching something in the distance. One of the* SENTRIES *is much younger than the other.*

SENTRY. Open those eyes of yours, lad. And drink it all in. You won't see something like this every day. This is an historic meeting.

YOUNG SENTRY. I dare say, but it's perishing cold. How long are they going to keep us hanging about?

SENTRY. We're sheltered by the wood here, but you can bet they're even colder than we are, out there in the plain.

YOUNG SENTRY. Look! They've come up to each other. I wonder what they're talking about?

SENTRY. What do you think they're talking about, mutton-head? Complaining about their chilblains? Inquiring how things are at home? The fate of the world, that's what they're arguing about. Things you and I won't ever understand. Even the words those bigwigs use—why, you wouldn't even know what they meant.

The SENTRIES *exit down* R *as—*

the LIGHTS BLACK-OUT *for a few moments*

When the LIGHTS *come up,* BECKET *and the* KING, *on horseback, are alone in the middle of the plain, facing each other.* BECKET *is* R *of the King. Throughout the episode the winter blizzard wails like a shrill dirge beneath their words. And during their silences only the wind is heard.*

KING. You look older, Thomas.

BECKET. You, too, Highness. Are you sure you aren't too cold?

KING. I'm frozen stiff. You love it, of course. You're in your element, aren't you? And you're barefooted, as well.

BECKET (*smiling*) That's my latest affectation.

KING. Even with these fur boots on, my chilblains are killing me. Aren't yours, or don't you have any?

BECKET (*gently*) Of course.

KING (*crackling*) You're offering them up to God, I hope, holy monk?

BECKET (*gravely*) I have better things to offer Him.

KING (*with a sudden cry*) If we start straight away, we're sure to quarrel. Let's talk about trivial things. You know my son is fourteen? He's come of age.

BECKET. Has he improved at all?

KING. He's a little idiot and sly like his mother. Becket, don't you ever marry.

BECKET (*smiling*) The matter has been taken out of my hands. By your Highness. It was you who had me ordained.

KING (*with a cry*) Let's not start yet, I tell you. Talk about something else.

BECKET (*lightly*) Has your Highness done much hunting lately?

KING (*snarling*) Yes, every day. And it doesn't amuse me any more.

BECKET. Have you any new hawks?

KING (*furiously*) The most expensive on the market. But they don't fly straight.

BECKET. And your horses?

KING. The Sultan sent me four superb stallions for the tenth anniversary of my reign. But they throw everyone. Nobody has managed to mount one of them, yet.

BECKET (*smiling*) I must see what I can do about that some day.

KING. They'll throw you, too. And we'll see your buttocks under your robe. At least, I hope so, or everything would be too dismal.

BECKET (*after a pause*) Do you know what I miss most, Sire? The horses.

KING. And the women?

BECKET (*simply*) I've forgotten.

KING. You hypocrite! You turned into a hypocrite when you became a priest. (*Abruptly*) Did you love Gwendolen?

BECKET. I've forgotten her, too.

KING. You did love her. That's the only way I can account for it.

BECKET (*gravely*) No, my prince, in my soul and conscience, I did not love her.

King. Then you never loved anything—that's worse. (*Churlishly*) Why are you calling me your prince, like in the old days?

Becket (*gently*) Because you have remained my prince.

King (*crying out*) Then why are you doing me harm?

Becket (*gently*) Let's talk about something else.

King. Well, what? I'm cold.

Becket. I always told you, my prince, that one must fight the cold with the cold's own weapons. Strip naked and splash yourself with cold water every morning.

King. I used to, when you were there to force me into it. I never wash now. I stink. I grew a beard at one time. Did you know?

Becket (*smiling*) Yes. I had a good laugh over it.

King. I cut it off, because it itched. (*He cries out suddenly, like a lost child*) Becket, I'm bored.

Becket (*gravely*) My prince. I do so wish I could help you.

King. Then what are you waiting for? You can see I'm dying for it.

Becket (*quietly*) I'm waiting for the honour of God and the honour of the King to become one.

King. You'll wait a long time, then.

Becket. Yes. I'm afraid I will.

(*There is a pause. Only the wind is heard*)

King (*suddenly*) If we've nothing more to say to each other, we might as well go and get warm.

Becket. We have everything to say to each other, my prince. The opportunity may not occur again.

King. Make haste, then. Or there'll be two frozen statues making their peace in a frozen eternity. I am your King, Becket. And so long as we are on this earth, you owe me the first move. I'm prepared to forget a lot of things, but not the fact that I am King. You yourself taught me that.

Becket (*gravely*) Never forget it, my prince. Even against God. You have a different task to do. You have to steer the ship.

King. And you—what do you have to do?

Becket. Resist you with all my might, when you steer against the wind.

King. Do you expect the wind to be behind me, Becket? No such luck! That's fairy-tale navigation. God on the King's side? That's never happened yet. It's a head-on wind. And there must be somebody to keep the watch.

Becket. And somebody else to direct the wind for God. The tasks have been shared out, once and for all. The pity of it is that it should have been between us two, my prince—who were friends.

King (*crossly*) The King of France—I still don't know what

he hopes to gain by it—preached at me for three whole days for me to make my peace with you. What good would it do you to provoke me beyond endurance?

BECKET. None.

KING. You know that I am the King, and that I must act like a King. What do you expect of me? Are you hoping I'll weaken?

BECKET. No. That would prostrate me.

KING. Do you hope to conquer me by force, then?

BECKET. You are the strong one.

KING. To win me around?

BECKET. No. Not that, either. It is not for me to win you round. I have only to say no to you.

KING. But you must be logical, Becket.

BECKET. No. That isn't necessary, my Liege. We must only do —absurdly—what we have been given to do—right to the end.

KING. I know you well enough, God knows. Ten years we spent together, little Saxon. At the hunt, at the whorehouse, at war; carousing all night long, the two of us; in the same girl's bed, sometimes. "Absurdly." That word isn't like you.

BECKET. Perhaps. I am no longer like myself.

KING (*derisively*) Have you been touched by grace?

BECKET (*gravely*) Not by the one you think. I am not worthy of it.

KING. Did you feel the Saxon in you coming out, despite papa's good collaborator's sentiments?

BECKET. No. Not that, either.

KING. What then?

BECKET. I felt for the first time that I was being entrusted with something, that's all—there in that empty cathedral, somewhere in France, that day when you ordered me to take up this burden. I was a man without honour. And suddenly I found it—one I never imagined would ever become mine—the honour of God. A frail, incomprehensible honour, vulnerable as a boy-king fleeing from danger.

KING (*roughly*) Suppose we talked a little more precisely, Becket, with words I understand? Otherwise we'll be here all night. I'm cold. And the others are waiting for us on the fringes of this plain.

BECKET. I am being precise.

KING. I'm an idiot, then. Talk to me like an idiot. That's an order. Will you agree to the twelve proposals which my Bishops have accepted in your absence at Northampton?

BECKET. No, Sire.

KING. Will you lift the excommunications which you pronounced on William of Aynsford and others of my liegemen?

BECKET. No, Sire, because that is the only weapon I have to defend this child, who was given, naked, into my care. (*He pauses*) Nor will I concede that the Bishops should forgo the right to appoint priests in their own dioceses, nor that church-men should be subject to any but the Church's jurisdiction. Those are my duties as a pastor—which it is not for me to relin-quish. But I shall agree to the nine other articles in a spirit of peace, and because I know that you must remain King—in all save the honour of God.

(*There is a pause*)

KING (*coldly*) Very well. I will help you defend your God, since that is your new vocation, in memory of the companion you once were to me—in all save the honour of the Realm. You may come back to England, Thomas.

BECKET. Thank you, my prince. I meant to go back in any case and give myself up to your power, for on this earth you are my King. And in all that concerns this earth I owe you obedience.

(*There is a pause*)

KING (*ill at ease*) Well, we've finished. Let's go back now. I'm cold.

BECKET (*dully*) I feel cold, too, now.

(*There is a pause. They look at each other. The wind howls*)

KING (*suddenly*) You never loved me, did you, Becket?

BECKET. In so far as I was capable of love, yes, my prince, I did.

KING. Did you start to love God? (*He cries out*) You mule! Can't you ever answer a simple question?

BECKET (*quietly*) I started to love the honour of God.

KING (*sombrely*) Come back to England. I give you my royal peace. May you find yours. And may you not discover you were wrong about yourself. This is the last time I shall come begging to you. (*He cries out*) I should never have seen you again. It hurts too much. (*His whole body is suddenly shaken by a sob*)

BECKET (*moving his horse nearer to the King; moved*) My prince . . .

KING (*moving his horse away; yelling*) No! No pity! It's dirty! Stand away from me. Go back to England. It's too cold out here.

BECKET (*gravely*) Farewell, my prince. Will you give me the kiss of peace?

KING. No! I can't bear to come near you. I can't bear to look at you. Later! Later! When it doesn't hurt any more.

BECKET. I shall set sail tomorrow. Farewell, my prince. I know I shall never see you again.

KING (*his face twisted with hatred*) How dare you say that to me after I gave you my royal word? Do you take me for a traitor?

(BECKET *looks gravely at the King for a few seconds, with a sort of pity in his eyes, then he slowly turns his horse and rides off up* R. *The wind howls*)

(*He calls*) Thomas!

> But BECKET *has not heard.*
> The KING *does not call a second time. He spurs his horse and gallops off up* L. *The wind howls as—*

the LIGHTS *dim to* BLACK-OUT

SCENE 3

SCENE—*King Henry's Palace in France.*

Two tables, at a close right-angle to each other, one up and down stage and one across it, are set LC. *Above the upstage table, the King's throne is* C *of it with two chairs* R *and* L *of the throne. A long bench is* L *of the table* L. *In the angle formed by the long tables there are two stools.*

When the LIGHTS *come up, the tables are set for dinner. The* QUEEN MOTHER *is standing in front of the chair* R *of the throne. The* YOUNG QUEEN *is standing in front of the chair* L *of the throne. The four* BARONS *are standing behind the bench* L *of the table* L. *The* YOUNGER PRINCE *is standing by a stool. Five* SERVANTS *are standing in a line* RC. *The* KING *enters up* R *with the* ELDER PRINCE, *and leads him* C. *The* SERVANTS *exit* R.

KING. Today, gentlemen, I shall not be the first to sit down. (*To the Elder Prince, with a comic bow*) You are the King, sir. The honour belongs to you. Take the high chair. Today I shall wait on *you.*

QUEEN MOTHER (*with slight irritation*) My son!

KING. I know what I'm doing, Madam! (*With a sudden shout to the Elder Prince*) Go on, you great loon, look sharp.

> (*The* ELDER PRINCE *flinches to avoid the blow he was expecting, then runs to the throne above the upstage table and stands, sly and rather ill at ease*)

Take your places, gentlemen. I shall remain standing.

> (*Everyone except the* KING *sits at the tables*)

Barons of England, here is your second King. Reviving an ancient custom, we have decided to have our successor crowned during our lifetime and to share our responsibilities with him. We ask you now to give him your homage and to honour him with the same title as ourself.

> (*The* BARONS *rise and lift their goblets and make a toast*)

BARONS (*together*) Long live the King! (*They drink, then resume their seats*)

(*The* KING *claps his hands.*

The SERVANTS *enter* R *with silver trays of food. The* 1ST SERVANT *puts his tray on the upstage table. The other* SERVANTS *cross to* L *of the table* L *and put their trays on it. All the* SERVANTS *then line up as before,* RC)

YOUNG QUEEN (*to the Elder Prince*) Sit up straight! And try to eat properly for once, now that you've been raised to glory.

KING (*grunting*) He hasn't the face for it. However, he'll be your King in good earnest one day, so you may as well get used to him. Besides, it's the best I had to offer.

QUEEN MOTHER (*indignantly*) My son! This game is unworthy of you and us. You insisted on playing it—at least play it with dignity.

KING (*rounding on her in fury*) I'll play the games that amuse me, Madam—(*he moves to* R *of the upstage table*) and I'll play them the way I choose. (*He moves to* R *of the table* L. *To the Barons*) This mummery, gentlemen, which is incidentally, without any importance at all—if your new King fidgets, let me know, I'll give him a good kick up his train—will at the very least have the appreciable result of showing our new friend the Archbishop that we can do without him. If there was one ancient privilege the Primacy clung to, tooth and nail, it was the exclusive right to annoint and consecrate the Kings of this Realm. Well, it will be that old toad the Bishop of York—(*he crosses below the table* L *and stands behind the Barons*) with letters from the Pope authorizing him to do so—I paid the price—who, tomorrow, will crown our son in our cathedral.

(*The* BARONS *look amazed at the King*)

What a joke that's going to be. (*He roars with laughter amid the general silence*) What a tremendous, marvellous joke! I'd give anything to see the Archbishop's face when he has to swallow that. (*He turns to the Elder Prince*) Get down from there, you imbecile! Go back to the bottom of the table where you belong and take your victuals with you. You aren't officially crowned until tomorrow.

(*The* ELDER PRINCE *picks up his plate, rises, moves to a stool and sits, casting a cowed, smouldering look at the King*)

(*Jovially, as he watches the Prince*) What a look! Filial sentiments are a fine thing to see, gentlemen. (*To the Elder Prince*) You'd like to be the real King, wouldn't you, you young pig? (*He moves up* L *of the tables*) You'd like that number "three" after your name,

eh, with papa good and stiff under his catafalque. You'll have
to wait a bit. Papa is well. Papa is very well indeed. (*He sits on
the throne*)

QUEEN MOTHER. My son, God knows I understand your
hatred of that man, but do not let it tempt you into making a
gesture you will regret, merely for the sake of wounding his
pride. Henry is still a child. Ambitious self-seekers may influence
him against you, may rouse a faction against you and use this
hasty coronation as a means of dividing the Kingdom.

KING. We are still alive, Madam, and in control. I let Becket
cheat me out of one or two articles the other day, but I had
something up my sleeve for him.

QUEEN MOTHER. Henry! I bore the weight of state affairs
longer than you have. I have been your Queen and I am your
mother. You are answerable for the interests of a great Kingdom.
It is England you must think of, not your hatred—or disappointed
love—for that man.

KING (*in a fury*) What gives you the right, Madam, to meddle
in my loves and hates?

QUEEN MOTHER (*rising*) You bear a rancour for that man
which is neither healthy nor manly. The King, your father, dealt
with his enemies more effectively. He had them killed and said no
more about it. Sweet Jesus, tear him out of your heart once and
for all. (*She bawls suddenly*) Oh, if I were a man!

KING (*grinning*) Thanks be to God, Madam, he gave you dugs.
Which I never personally benefited from. I suckled a peasant
girl.

QUEEN MOTHER (*acidly*) No doubt that is why you have remained so lumpish, my son. (*She resumes her seat*)

YOUNG QUEEN. And haven't I a say in the matter, sir?
Becket! Always Becket! I am your wife and your Queen. (*She
rises*) I refuse to be treated like this. I shall complain to my father
the Duke of Aquitaine. I shall complain to my uncle the Emperor.
I shall complain to all the Kings of Europe, my cousins. I shall
complain to God!

KING (*shouting rather vulgarly*) I should start with God. Be off
to your private chapel, Madam, and see if He's at home. (*He
turns to the Queen Mother*) And you, the other Madam, away to
your chamber with your secret councillors and go and spin your
webs. Get out, both of you! I can't stand the sight of you! I retch
with boredom whenever I set eyes on you. And young Henry the
Third, too! Go on, get out! (*He rises*)

(*The* QUEEN MOTHER *and the* PRINCES *rise.*
The YOUNG QUEEN *exits up* R. *The* QUEEN MOTHER *scurries off
after her with a great rustle of silk. The* PRINCES *cross up* R)

(*He yells*) Here's my royal foot in your royal buttocks. (*He kicks the Princes up* R) And to the devil with my whole family, if he'll have you!

(*The* PRINCES *run out up* R)

(*To the Servants*) Get out, all of you! Get out! Get out! Get out!

(*The* SERVANTS *exit up* R)

(*He moves to the upstage end of the table* L. *More calmly*) Let us drink, gentlemen. That's about all one can do in your company. (*He picks up his goblet*) Let us get drunk, like men, all night— (*he moves to* R *of the table* L) until we roll under the table, in vomit and oblivion. (*He fills the Barons' goblets and leans over the table to them*) Ah, my four idiots! My faithful hounds. It's warm beside you, like being in a stable. Good sweat! Comfortable nothingness. (*He taps their skulls*) Not the least little glimmer inside to spoil the fun. (*He straightens up*) And to think that before he came I was like you. A good fat machine for belching after drink, for pee-ing, for mounting girls and punching heads. What the devil did you put into it, Becket, to stop the wheels from going round? (*He moves to* R *of the upstage table. Suddenly, to the* 2ND BARON) Tell me, do you think sometimes?

2ND BARON (*leaning forward*) Never, Sire. Thinking has never agreed with an Englishman. It's unhealthy.

KING (*suddenly quite calm*) Drink up. (*He moves and sits in his throne*)

(*The* BARONS *rise, and group around the King. The* 1ST BARON *refills the King's goblet and the* 2ND BARON *refills the other goblets*)

That's always been considered a healthy thing to do. Has Becket landed?

(*There is a pause*)

I'm told the sea has been too rough to cross these last few days.

1ST BARON (*sombrely*) He has landed, Sire, despite the sea.

KING. Where?

1ST BARON. On a deserted stretch of coast, near Sandwich.

(*The* BARONS *resume their seats*)

KING. So God did not choose to drown him?

1ST BARON. No.

KING (*in his sly, brutish way*) Was nobody there waiting for him? There must be one or two men in England whom he can't call his friends.

1ST BARON. Yes. Gervase and Regnault were lying in wait for him, but the Dean of Oxford went to meet them and charged them not to cause bloodshed and make you look a traitor, as you had given the Archbishop a safe conduct.

King (*soberly*) Yes, I gave him a safe conduct.

1st Baron. All along the road to Canterbury, the peasants, the artisans and the small shopkeepers came out to meet him, armed and cheering him and escorting him from village to village. Not a single Noble, not a single Norman showed his face.

King. Only the Saxons?

1st Baron. Poor people armed with makeshift shields and rusty lances. Riff-raff. Swarms of them, though, all encamped around Canterbury, to protect him. (*Gloomily*) Who would have thought there were so many people in England.

King. A miserable wretch who ate my bread! A fellow I raised up from nothing. A Saxon! A man I loved. (*He shouts like a madman*) Yes, I loved him! And I believe I still do! Enough, oh God! Enough! Stop, stop, oh God, I've had enough! (*He flings himself across the table, sobbing hysterically*)

(*The* Barons, *stupefied, rise and group round the King*)

1st Baron (*timidly*) Your Highness . . .

King. I can do nothing! Nothing! I'm as limp and useless as a girl! I tremble before him astonished. And I am the King. (*With a sudden cry*) Will no one rid me of him? A priest! A priest who jeers at me and does me injury. Are there none but cowards like myself around me? Are there no men left in England? Oh, my heart! My heart is beating too fast to bear! (*He lies still as death*)

(*The four* Barons *stand around speechless. Suddenly on a percussion instrument, there rises a rhythmic beating, a sort of muffled tom-tom which is at first only the agitated heart-beats of the King, but which swells and grows more insistent.*

The Barons *look at each other, then they straighten, buckle their sword-belts, pick up their helmets and exit slowly up* R, *leaving the* King *alone with the muffled rhythm of the heart-beats, which will continue until the murder. The* King *lies across the table in the deserted hall for a while then sits up and looks around, sees the Barons have gone and suddenly realizes why. A wild, lost look comes into his eyes. There is a moment's pause, then he collapses with a long, broken moan*)

Oh, my Thomas!

the Lights *dim to* Black-out

SCENE 4

SCENE—*Canterbury Cathedral.*

The stone slab down R *is now an altar. There is a stand down* LC *on which hang the Archbishop's robes, mitre, etc.*

When the LIGHTS *come up the heart-beats are still heard.* BECKET *is down* L. *The* LITTLE MONK *is* R *of Becket, helping him on with his vestments.*

BECKET. I must look my best today. Make haste.

MONK. It's difficult with all those little laces. It wants a girl's hands.

BECKET (*softly*) A man's hands are better, today. Never mind the laces. The alb, quickly. And the stole. And then the cope.

MONK (*conscientiously*) If it's worth doing it's worth doing well.

BECKET. You're quite right. If it's worth doing it's worth doing well. Do up all the little laces, every one of them. God will give us time.

  (*There is a pause. The* MONK *struggles manfully on, putting out his tongue in his concentration. The throbbing grows louder*)

(*He smiles*) Don't put your tongue out like that.

MONK (*sweating but content*) There. That's all done. But I'd rather have cleaned out our pigsty at home. It's not half such hard work.

BECKET. Now the alb.

  (*The* MONK *collects the alb from the stand and helps* BECKET *to put it on*)

Were you fond of your pigs?

MONK (*his eyes lighting up*) Yes, I was. (*He hands the stole to Becket*)

BECKET (*putting on the stole*) At my father's house, we had some pigs, too, when I was a child. (*He smiles*) We're two rough lads from Hastings, you and I. Give me the chasuble.

  (*The* MONK *hands the chasuble to Becket*)

(*He kisses the chasuble and slips it over his head. Gently*) Do you miss your knife?

MONK. Yes. (*He pauses*) Will it be today?

BECKET (*gravely*) I think so, my son. Are you afraid.

MONK. Oh, no. Not if we have time to fight. All I want is the chance to strike a few blows first; so I shan't have done nothing but receive them all my life. If I can kill one Norman first—just one, I don't want much—one for one, that will seem fair and right enough to me.

(*The* Monk *helps* Becket *to don his cope*)

Becket (*with a kindly smile*) Are you so very set on killing one?
Monk. One for one. That's what justice means, isn't it?

(Becket *smiles and does not answer*)

Becket. Give me the mitre.

(*The* Monk *collects the mitre and hands it to Becket*)

(*He puts on the mitre. Quietly*) Oh, Lord, You forbade Peter to
strike a blow in the Garden of Olives. But I shall not deprive this
lad of that joy. He has had too few joys in his short span on earth.
(*To the monk*) Now fetch me my silver cross. I must hold it.

(*The* Monk *exits* L *and re-enters immediately with a silver cross*)

Monk (*handing the cross to Becket*) Lord, it's heavy. A good swipe
with that and they'd feel it. My word, I wish I could have it.
Becket (*stroking the Monk's head*) Lucky little Saxon! This
black world will have been in order to the end, for you.

(*The* Monk *takes the clothes stand and exits* L)

(*Gravely*) There. I'm ready, all adorned for Your festivities,
Lord. Do not, in this interval of waiting, let one last doubt enter
my soul.
(*There is a loud knocking off up* L.
   A Priest *runs wildly in up* L)

Priest (*running to* R *of Becket*) Your Grace! There are four
armed men outside! I've barricaded the door, but they're break-
ing it in. Quickly! You must go into the back of the church and
have the choir gates closed.
Becket (*calmly*) It is time for Vespers, William. Does one close
the choir gates during Vespers? I never heard of such a thing.

(*The* Monk *enters* L)

Priest (*nonplussed*) I know, but . . .
Becket. Everything must be the way it should be. The choir
gates will remain open. (*To the Monk*) Come, boy, let us go up to
the altar. This is no place to be.

(Becket *and the* Monk *move to the stone slab down* R. *There is
a great crash off* L.
   The four Barons *enter up* L *and draw their swords.* Becket *turns
to face them, grave and calm. They stop a moment, uncertain and
disconcerted, four statues, huge and threatening. The heart-beats cease.
There is a heavy silence*)

(*Simply*) Here it comes. The supreme folly. This is its hour.
(*He holds their eyes*)

(*The* BARONS *dare not move*)

(*Coldly*) One does not enter armed into God's house. What do you want?

1ST BARON (*thickly*) Your death.

(*There is a pause*)

2ND BARON (*thickly*) You bring shame to the King.

BECKET (*softly*) It is time for the service. (*He turns to face* R, *without paying any further attention to them*)

(*The muffled throbbing recommences. The* BARONS *close in like automata. The* MONK *suddenly leaps forward, grabs the silver cross and brandishes it in order to protect Becket, but one of the* BARONS *swings his sword and fells him to the ground*)

Not even one. It would have given him so much pleasure, Lord. (*With a sudden cry*) Oh, how difficult You make it all. And how heavy Your Honour is to bear. (*Quietly*) Poor Henry.

The BARONS *hurl themselves on to* BECKET, *who falls at the first blow. They hack at the body, grunting like woodcutters.*

The PRIEST *flees off* R, *with a long scream which echoes in the empty cathedral. The heart-beats cease as—*

the LIGHTS *dim to* BLACK-OUT

When the LIGHTS *come up, the altar cloth has been removed and the slab is again the tomb. The* KING, *dressed as at the opening of the play, is on his knees at the slab. Four* MONKS *are whipping him with ropes, almost duplicating the gestures of the Barons as they killed Becket.*

KING (*crying out*) Are you satisfied now, Becket? Does this settle our account? Has the honour of God been washed clean?

(*The* MONKS *finish beating the King, kneel and bow their heads. The* KING *mutters; one feels it is part of the ceremony*)

Thank you. Yes, yes, of course, it was agreed. I forgive you. Many thanks. (*He collapses over the slab*)

(*The* MONKS *rise and exit up* R. *Organ music is heard.*

The PAGE *enters* L *with a vast robe and the King's clothes. He crosses to the King, wraps the robe around him, puts the clothes on the slab then exits* R.

The 2ND BARON *enters down* R.

The 3RD BARON *enters up* C.

The 4TH BARON *enters down* L. *The* KING *rises. The* BARONS *help him to dress. He dresses hurriedly with evident bad temper*)

(*He grimaces ill-humouredly and growls*) The pigs! The Norman bishops just went through the motions, but those little Saxon monks—my word, they had their money's worth.

(*The* 1ST BARON *enters up* L *and crosses to* C. *A joyful peal of bells is heard and the sound of cheering crowds*)

1ST BARON. Sire! Sire! The operation has been successful. The Saxon mob is cheering outside the Cathedral, acclaiming your Majesty's name in the same breath as Becket's. If the Saxons are on our side now, Prince Henry's followers have lost the day.

KING (*with a touch of hypocritical majesty beneath his slightly loutish manner*) The honour of God, gentlemen, is a very good thing, and taken all in all, one gains by having it on one's side. Thomas Becket, who was our friend, used to say so. England will owe her ultimate victory over chaos to him and it is our wish that, henceforward, he should be honoured and prayed to in this Kingdom as a Saint.

(*The* BARONS *kneel*)

(*He crosses to* C) Come, gentlemen. We will determine, tonight, in Council, what posthumous honours to render him and what punishment to deal out to his murderers.

1ST BARON (*imperturbably*) Sire, they are unknown.

KING (*impenetrably*) Our justice will seek them out, Baron, and you will be specially entrusted with this enquiry, so that no one will be in any doubt as to our Royal desire to defend the honour of God and the memory of our friend from this day forward.

The organ swells triumphantly, mingled with the sound of the bells and the cheering crowds. The BARONS *rise.*

The KING *and the* BARONS *exit up* L *as—*

the CURTAIN *falls*

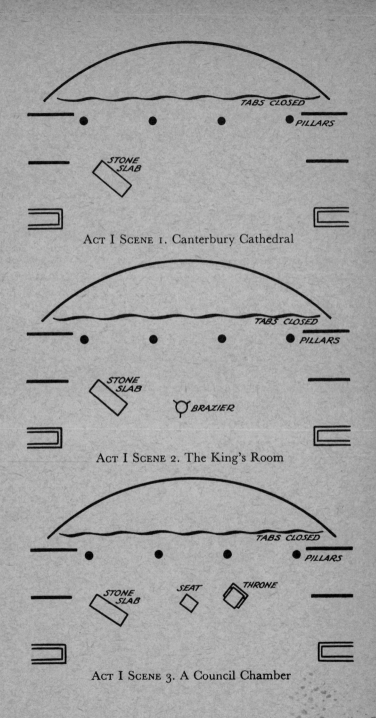

ACT I SCENE 1. Canterbury Cathedral

ACT I SCENE 2. The King's Room

ACT I SCENE 3. A Council Chamber

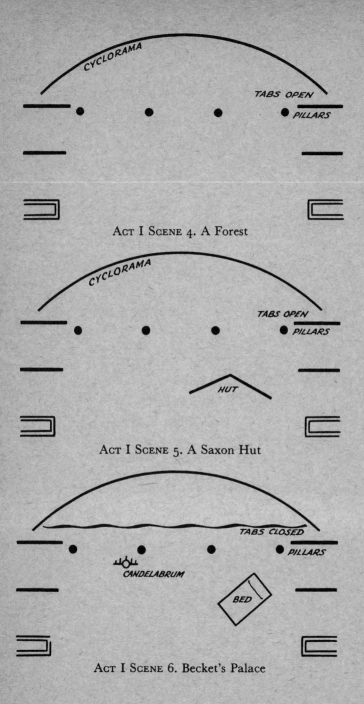

Act I Scene 4. A Forest

Act I Scene 5. A Saxon Hut

Act I Scene 6. Becket's Palace

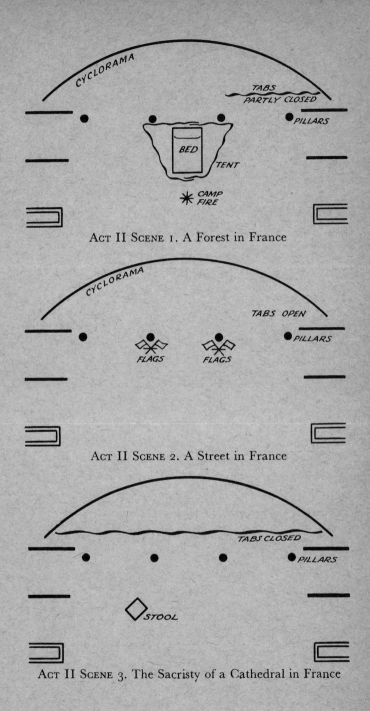

ACT II SCENE 1. A Forest in France

ACT II SCENE 2. A Street in France

ACT II SCENE 3. The Sacristy of a Cathedral in France

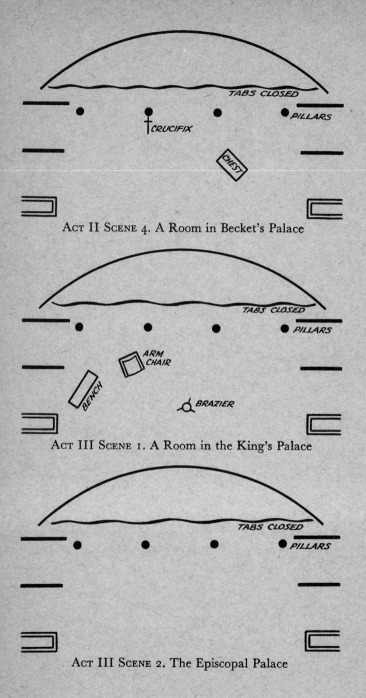

TABS CLOSED

PILLARS

† CRUCIFIX

CHEST

ACT II SCENE 4. A Room in Becket's Palace

TABS CLOSED

PILLARS

ARM CHAIR

BENCH

BRAZIER

ACT III SCENE 1. A Room in the King's Palace

TABS CLOSED

PILLARS

ACT III SCENE 2. The Episcopal Palace

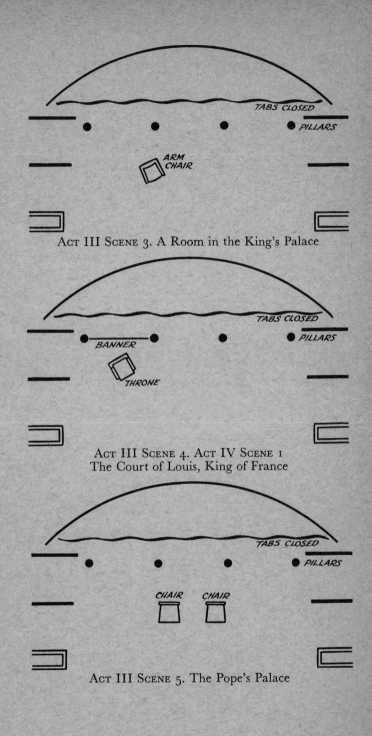

ACT III SCENE 3. A Room in the King's Palace

ACT III SCENE 4. ACT IV SCENE 1
The Court of Louis, King of France

ACT III SCENE 5. The Pope's Palace

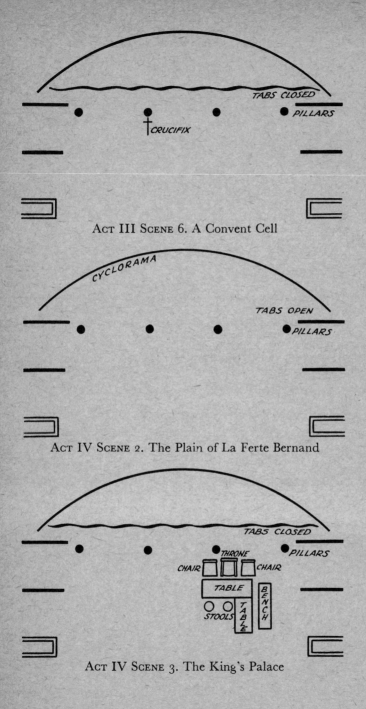

ACT III SCENE 6. A Convent Cell

ACT IV SCENE 2. The Plain of La Ferte Bernand

ACT IV SCENE 3. The King's Palace

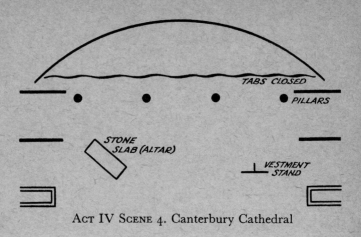

ACT IV SCENE 4. Canterbury Cathedral

The settings shown in this Acting Edition are the same in basic requirements as those used in the London Production of the play. Only the decorative elements of the background have been simplified as these required considerable stage machinery to operate them. A permanent line of pillars, supporting arches, is now shown across the stage. Different sets of Tabs can be used behind these to suggest the differing locales

FURNITURE AND PROPERTY LIST

ACT I

SCENE 1

On stage—Stone slab (down R)
Off stage—King's clothes (PAGE)
        Large white towel (PAGE)
Personal—KING: crown, robe

SCENE 2

On stage—Stone slab (down R)
        Brazier and logs (down C)

SCENE 3

Strike—Brazier, logs and towel
Set—Seat C
    Throne LC
Off stage—Tray with food (1ST SOLDIER)
Personal—KING: seal
        ARCHBISHOP: ring

SCENE 4

Strike—Stone slab from down R
      Seat C
      Throne
Set—Branches from flies
Off stage—6 "Hobby horses" (BARONS, KING and BECKET)
        2 hawks (KING and BECKET)

SCENE 5

Set—Hut (LC) *In it:* pile of rags
Off stage—Load of wood (SAXON MAN)
        Bowl of water (SAXON MAN)
        Bloodstained cloth (BECKET)
        Gourd of juniper-juice (BECKET)
Personal—BECKET: dagger, purse
        KING: riding-crop
        BOY: knife

SCENE 6

On stage—Low bed-couch. *On it:* cushions, fur coverlet, stringed instrument
        Candelabrum
Off stage—Fork (1ST BARON)

81

ACT II

SCENE 1

On stage—Branches from flies
    Fire (down C)
    Food (for Barons)
    Tent (C) *In it:* bed with bedding, the King's shirt
    Tent (L)
Off stage—Knife (1ST SOLDIER)

SCENE 2

Strike—Tents and fire
On stage—Flags

SCENE 3

Strike—Flags and standards
Off stage—Stool (CHOIRBOY)
    Letter (1ST SOLDIER)
Personal—BARONS: swords

SCENE 4

Strike—Stool
Set—Chest with clothes LC and fur coverlet
  On pillar: crucifix

ACT III

SCENE 1

On stage—Bench (down R) *On it:* tapestry work for the Young Queen
    Armchair (RC) *On it:* tapestry work for the Queen Mother
    Tapestries (R and L of pillars)
    Brazier (down C)
Off stage—Cup-and-ball (KING)
    Cord for cats' cradles (PRINCES)
    Letter (ETIENNE)
    Seal (ETIENNE)

SCENE 2

Personal—BECKET: ring

SCENE 3

Setting as Act III, Scene 1

SCENE 4

On stage—Banners up RC
    Throne (RC)
Off stage—Parchment (FOLLIOT)

SCENE 5

Strike—Throne and banners
Set—2 gilt throne-chairs (C)

SCENE 6

Strike—2 throne-chairs
Set—*On Pillar:* crucifix
Off stage—Cross for carving and knife (LITTLE MONK)

ACT IV

SCENE 1

Setting as Act III, Scene 4
Personal—LOUIS: letter

SCENE 2

No properties

SCENE 3

On stage—2 tables. *On them:* platters, goblets, flasks of wine
        Throne
        2 chairs
        Bench
        2 stools
Off stage—5 silver trays with food (SERVANTS)

SCENE 4

Set—Stone slab (down R) dressed as altar
    Stand with Archbishop's robes and mitre
Off stage—Silver cross (MONK)
During BLACK-OUT
Strike—Altar dressing
Off stage—4 whipping ropes (MONKS)

LIGHTING PLOT

Property Fittings Required—brazier fire, candelabra

ACT I SCENE 1
Interior. A Cathedral
    THE APPARENT SOURCE OF LIGHT IS—a window up RC
    THE MAIN ACTING AREA IS—at a tomb C

To open:	The stage in darkness	
Cue 1	After rise of CURTAIN	(page 1)
	Bring up lights for effect of sunlight through stained-glass windows	
Cue 2	The KING kneels at tomb	(page 1)
	Fade lights except for a spotlight on the King	
Cue 3	KING: ". . . understand each other."	(page 1)
	Bring up spotlight on Becket LC	
Cue 4	KING: ". . . praying at the moment."	(page 2)
	Fade spotlight on Becket	
Cue 5	KING: ". . . at than me."	(page 2)
	Fade spotlight on King	

SCENE 2
Interior. The King's Room
THE MAIN ACTING AREAS ARE—C, down C and down R

Cue 6	Follows previous cue	(page 2)
	Bring up general lighting for daylight effect	
	Brazier switched on	
Cue 7	BECKET and the KING exit	(page 6)
	Dim to BLACK-OUT	

SCENE 3
Interior. A Council Chamber
THE MAIN ACTING AREAS ARE—C, LC, down L and down R

Cue 8	When Scene set	(page 6)
	Bring up lights	
Cue 9	The BISHOPS exit	(page 11)
	Dim to BLACK-OUT	

SCENE 4
Exterior. A Forest
THE MAIN ACTING AREA IS—down C

Cue 10	When Scene set	(page 12)
	Bring up lights	
Cue 11	The BARONS exit R	(page 12)
	Flash of lightning	
Cue 12	After peal of thunder	(page 13)
	Dim to BLACK-OUT	

SCENE 5
Interior. A Saxon Hut
THE MAIN ACTING AREA IS—C of the hut

Cue 13	When Scene set	(page 13)
	Bring up lights	

Cue 25   Becket exits   (page 48)
              Dim lights to Black-out

              Scene 3
Interior. The King's Palace
Cue 26   When Scene set   (page 49)
              Bring up lights as Act III, Scene 1
              Brazier on

              Scene 4
Interior. A Palace Room
The Main Acting Areas are—rc and c
Cue 27   When Scene set   (page 51)
              Bring up lights
Cue 28   Louis: "The man needs money."   (page 54)
              Dim lights to Black-out

              Scene 5
Interior. The Pope's Palace
The Main Acting Area is—c
Cue 29   When Scene set   (page 55)
              Bring up lights
Cue 30   Pope: ". . . of good advice."   (page 57)
              Dim lights to Black-out

              Scene 6
Interior. A Convent Cell
The Main Acting Area is—c
Cue 31   When Scene set   (page 57)
              Bring up lights c

ACT IV Scene 1
Interior. A Palace Room
To open: Lighting as Act III, Scene 4
Cue 32   Becket: ". . . talk to him."   (page 60)
              Dim lights to Black-out

              Scene 2
Exterior. A Plain
The Main Acting Areas are—c and down r
Cue 33   When Scene set   (page 60)
              Bring up lights
Cue 34   The Sentries exit   (page 60)
              Dim lights to Black-out
Cue 35   When Becket and King on stage   (page 60)
              Bring up lights
Cue 36   The King exits   (page 65)
              Dim lights to Black-out

              Scene 3
Interior. The Palace Room
The Main Acting Area is—lc
Cue 37   When Scene set   (page 65)
              Bring up lights
Cue 38   King: "Oh, my Thomas!"   (page 69)
              Dim lights to Black-out

SCENE 4
Interior. A Cathedral

Cue 39	When Scene set	(page 70)
	Bring up lights	
Cue 40	BECKET is murdered	(page 72)
	Dim lights to BLACK-OUT	
Cue 41	Follows above cue	(page 72)
	Bring up lights as at the opening of Act I, Scene 1	

EFFECTS PLOT

ACT I

SCENE 1

Cue 1   At rise of CURTAIN   (page 1)
Crowd noises

Cue 2   KING: ". . . to flog me."   (page 1)
Crowd noises fade

SCENE 2

No cues

SCENE 3

No cues

SCENE 4

Cue 3   When Lights come up   (page 12)
Sound of hunting-horns

Cue 4   The KING enters   (page 12)
Peal of thunder followed by the sound of torrential rain

Cue 5   KING: "Here comes the deluge."   (page 12)
Peal of thunder

Cue 6   KING: ". . . with hawks?"   (page 12)
Fade rain slightly

Cue 7   BECKET: ". . . a right to it."   (page 12)
Stop rain

Cue 8   KING: ". . . have a shape?"   (page 12)
Rain recommences

Cue 9   The KING exits   (page 13)
Sound of hunting-horns

Cue 10   After lightning flash   (page 13)
Peal of thunder

SCENE 5

Cue 11   When lights come up   (page 13)
Sound of rain ceases

Cue 12   At end of Scene   (page 18)
Sound of hunting-horns

SCENE 6

Cue 13   When lights come up   (page 19)
Sounds of singing and laughter

Cue 14   BECKET: "Go on playing."   (page 19)
Reduce sounds of singing and laughter

Cue 15   KING: "Get up."   (page 20)
The sounds of banqueting fade

ACT II

SCENE 1

Cue 16   At end of Scene   (page 35)
Sound of bells. This continues into the next scene

SCENE 2

Cue 17   When lights come up   (page 35)
Sound of crowd and trumpets

Any character costumes or wigs needed in the performance of this play can be hired from Charles H Fox Ltd, 25 Shelton Street, London WC2H 9HX.

PRINTED IN GREAT BRITAIN BY
BUTLER & TANNER LTD.,
FROME AND LONDON